S0-AGF-251

SAVE PENNIES, BANK MILLIONS

ACCELERATE FINANCIAL GROWTH ON A MODEST INCOME

Helsa Ariass
and
Glaurys Ariass

WITHDRAWN

®

ARIASS FORTUNE, INC.
Publishing House
A division of Ariass Fortune, Inc.

SAVE PENNIES, BANK MILLIONS

ACCELERATE FINANCIAL GROWTH ON A MODEST INCOME

Copyright © 1998 by Helsa Ariass and Glaurys Ariass
Cover Photograph "Penny Chess Moves" Copyright © 1998

For mail orders, write:

Ariass Fortune, Inc.
P.O. Box 6590
Beverly Hills, CA 90212

For on-line orders, visit:

http://www.ariassfortune.com

All rights reserved. This book, or parts thereof, may not be reproduced
under any circumstances without written authorization.

Published by Ariass Fortune, Inc.

Printed in the United States of America
Library of Congress Catalogue in Publication Data

ISBN 0-9664584-0-0
Library of Congress Catalogue Number   98-92854

ARIASS FORTUNE, INC.
TM and ® designate trademarks and registered trademarks of Ariass Fortune, Inc.

ACKNOWLEDGEMENTS

We thank and praise our Lord and Savior Jesus Christ for lovingly guiding and steering us in the direction we should go. We also thank the Lord for blessing us with so many beautiful people, and allowing them to share so much wisdom and knowledge in our 'walks of life'.

Special thanks to the following collaborators:

Marty Gilliland
Gilliland Printing
Aliso Viejo, California

Scott Cooper, President
Herrington Management, Inc.
Irvine, California

Eartha V. Moore
Serrano 105 Publishing Co.
Beverly Hills, California

PREFACE

Although this book was written as a result of the thoughts and inspiration of two individuals, it is written in first person.

"I don't have fifty dollars!" Oftentimes, conversations with friends and family ended on a similar note. "I have a few pennies, a multitude of bills, and I'm overdrawn fifty dollars. But I don't have fifty dollars. So where am I going to get fifty dollars to save? I can't afford it." Yet time after time, our resolve was that certainly circumstances would eventually change. Thinking about how they would change was more unsettling than facing the fact that things would not change at all. Indeed, a change needed to take place, but we couldn't sit around and wait for it. We had to make it happen somehow. If things were going to get better, we were going to have to be the catalysts. We were going to have to do something to make it better. So we did.

The first thing that needed to change was the mindset, and then the approach. Somehow we understood and agreed that doing the same thing over and over again, expecting a different result, was a mild case of insanity. So we devised and implemented certain systems and controls and tested them in our own financial environment. Once we began doing things differently, the results changed drastically. Thereupon, friends, family, and business associates incorporated the same financial principles. For the first time, we, along with all our friends started to enjoy a financial stability. Even business associates, with whom we shared this system, noticed impressive percent of net worth increase on a monthly basis.

This inspired us to write this book. We want to share this system with everyone who is willing to subject himself to a sound discipline in pursuit of financial betterment.

A NOTE FROM THE AUTHORS

SAVE PENNIES, BANK MILLIONS. From childhood we are conditioned, if not programmed, to chase after the big dollars and throw away the small change, the pennies. "For the plans I have in mind, I'm going to need millions; pennies won't do. Pennies are just not enough." So considering our future endeavors and business projections, we don't waste time collecting "pennies," the little and petty things. Instead, we incessantly go after the "millions," the big and significant things, the things that make a difference. We all know that pennies add up to dollars, one or a million the same. Yet to our disadvantage, we ignorantly subscribe to the philosophy that we don't need our pennies to attain a million dollars.

That reminds us of the bee-swatting old man, who always complained about his failing honey production company. Everyone called him Ol' Combs. All his life, he tried to get his business "off the floor." But the Comb's Honey Co. never went beyond mediocrity, until he gave it to his

---

grandson for his 30th birthday. In two years, the Comb's Honey Co. became a multi-million dollar company. By the way, Ol' Comb's grandson was a beekeeper, not a bee-swatter.

If you don't save pennies, you certainly won't bank millions. Remember, he who exercises good stewardship over the little things, enjoys the big things. On that note, if you save and build on the "little," you'll make and bank "much." Hence, the title.

TABLE OF CONTENTS

1

THE SIGNIFICANCE OF CREDIT

Penny Tip:

Always honor your Word.
If you breach your own Word,
who won't you breach?

Before you can begin to build an empire, you must clean your credit. More often than not, credit cleaning has nothing to do with having disposable lump sums of money. If that were indeed the case, then all millionaires would have excellent credit. The reality is that many millionaires have horrible credit ratings, and even end up bankrupt. Yes! Bankrupt Millionaires. There is such a class of people who file bankruptcy but get to keep their millions. "Well what's wrong with that?" Unless you are going to carry around with all your cash in the event of every purchase, you are better off with credit. You probably wouldn't mind carrying cash to purchase a sandwich or maybe an appliance such as a toaster. In fact, most people usually do because saving $200 is not a big feat to accomplish. In the course of our lives, most of us have learned to exercise the necessary patience to save two or three hundred dollars to buy an item. However, when purchasing a computer, a car, or a house, we are more reluctant to pay on a cash basis, not to mention carry around with that amount of money. The preferable form of payment is credit.

Credit is trust placed on you at the point of sale. The vendor trusts that you will pay him in increments of a specified amount at a specific point in time. The likelihood that someone with a good credit rating will adhere to the terms of a credit agreement is greater than that of someone with poor credit rating. Therefore, an individual with bad credit, despite any stash of cash he may have, has limited options for forms of payments, thereby limited access to certain commodities in society. That simply means that he is not considered a trustworthy consumer in the eyes of most financial institutions. Nobody believes that he will honor his word to pay for services. Good credit is less about money and more about "good word" and honesty.

A good friend of mine, who happens to have all of his money in an offshore account, is a millionaire three times over. But his credit rating is atrocious. He couldn't convince anyone to extend him credit even if he offered to pay twice the amount. Why? Because his previous credit history indicates that he has not been responsible adhering to credit terms. On a vacation to California, one incident comes to mind when he went on a shopping spree, paying all in cash of course. After buying practically every souvenir he set eyes on, the evening came to a halting end when he tried to rent a nice jet black Toyota 4WD truck with which he hoped to cruise the streets of Los Angeles. At that point, he was forced to face the grim reality that he was no longer a privileged consumer; and all his money could not change that fact. He offered to pay in cash three times the required deposit for the rental of the truck. Yet, his offer was declined. The auto rental company wanted a valid credit card before it released the vehicle to him.

At the time, I was a struggling student at UCLA, trying to make ends meet. I was making $6.75 an hour at the ASUCLA Student Finance Department. My net worth probably consisted of a typewriter and five Cup-o-Noodle Soups sitting on my kitchen counter. I certainly did not have the kind of money he did. But I had excellent credit. With great embarrassment, he asked me whether I would lend him my credit for the rental of his truck. He thought the whole scenario was rather ridiculous and unnecessary. After all, he was indeed a very wealthy individual being subjected to such public humiliation. It was all very stupid in his opinion. Yet it was all very clear to me. I was privileged with certain commodities because of my past record of making my word good, and he was not. Although the "cash only" basis is an attractive method of payment, it's just not supported by today's financial structure.

When you contract a service, you are in essence stating that you have set aside monies and/or have the resources to pay for such service. You may either pay upon the rendering of service or a later date billing. Either way, the vendor is assuming that whether you pay now or later, you have already set funds aside to cover the agreed partial payment amounts or full cost of his service or product. We all know that you can not make payments to anyone without money. But more importantly than having money, the vendor wants assurance that he will be paid, before he provides a service. At that point, the issue is not whether or not you have money. The issue is whether or not the vendor trusts you will pay. While having money is good, only good credit assures the vendor that you will indeed pay him. For your own good, don't use services for which you have not set monies aside. I know what you're thinking. "What's the point of using credit, if I have to have the money set aside in advance?"

At the risk of losing your interest, the blunt truth is that credit is not really "buy now and pay later," that's just one of the advantages. Credit is your Word. If you breach your word and you don't pay, your credit is rated poorly. Conversely, if you keep your word and pay, your credit is rated excellently. With each respective rating, come certain restrictions or privileges. So, keep your word, and build your credit.

2

HOW TO CLEAN YOUR DIRTY CREDIT

Penny Tip:

Don't run away from creditors;
pay your debts off.

Get a copy of your credit rating report by calling or writing to one of the following:

EQUIFAX
P.O. Box 740241
Atlanta, GA 30374-0241
(800) 997-2493
http://www.equifax.com

EXPERIAN
P.O. Box 2104
Allen, TX 75013-2104
(888) 397-3742
http://www.experian.com

TRANS UNION
P.O. Box 390
Springfield, PA 19064-0390
(714) 738-3800
(213) 620-8530
http://www.tuc.com

Whatever appears on this report is what all merchants, vendors and inquiring parties will see. Based on this report they will decide whether or not to do business with you. So don't leave your credit rating to chance. Find out how the finacial sector rates you, and if poorly, change it.

Write to one of the credit agencies listed above. Make sure you include your full name, address, social security number, date of birth, and a copy of your driver's license. If you do not have a driver's license, include a valid ID and copy of a utility bill that confirms your address. They will usually give you one complimentary credit rating. Otherwise, there may be a small fee of approximately $20.00 for a credit rating report. However, if you have been denied credit or employment because of your credit rating, you may be entitled to a free report. At any rate, it behooves you to know what has been reported on your record to ensure against erroneous reporting or fraudulent activity in your name. See sample letter provided later in this chapter.

When you receive your report, mark the past due balances that you can pay off immediately, preferably the smaller ones first. Contact the creditors at the addresses reported on the credit report and pay them. Then contact the creditors for the larger amounts, and make arrangements for partial payments. In a later chapter, we will discuss proper budgeting skills that will enable you to make these partial payments.

Creditors are more than willing to work with you. In fact, after not hearing from you for such a long time regarding their money, they are elated that you thought about clearing your account with them. If a creditor is no longer in business, that is not an excuse to not pay for a service

10

that you used. Keep in mind that you are trying to clean your credit, not get away with not paying. Do your due diligence in locating the vendors with whom you have a delinquent accounts and make arrangements for payment. In most cases, you can clean your own credit without spending money on "Credit Clean Scams." Granted, some cases are more complex than others. Should this be your case, The National Foundation for Consumer Credit has agencies that can help you. You may call (800) 388-2227 for the address and telephone number of the office nearest you. But for all intensive purposes, you can do it yourself.

If anything on your report seems fraudulent or otherwise inaccurate, write to the credit bureau and request an investigation immediately. As a consumer, you have rights to dispute any inaccuracies. Exercise your rights.

I know this stage can be a little intimidating and embarrassing, but don't allow yourself to fall into such pit of emotions. If you are ever going to become a financial empire, you must be focused and determined to press beyond intimidation and embarrassment. It is important that you accomplish this step. If you give up here, you have given up on your financial success. And honestly, nobody will care that you didn't achieve anything other than failure. This temporary discomfort can be crippling, but no more than a lifetime's struggle. Allow me to encourage you towards financial health.

Sample letter to send Credit Services

Broke D. Joe
0000 Nowhere Lane
Debt city, Any State 00000

April 10, 1998

TRW IS&S-NCAC
P.O. Box 2105
Allen, TX 75013-9505

Dear Sir or Madam:

Please accept this letter as a formal request for a complimentary credit rating report. My personal information is as follows:

Full Name:	Broke Down Joe
Address:	0000 Nowhere Lane
	Debt city, Any State 00000
SS#:	000-00-0000
Date of Birth:	1/31/75

I have included a copy of my driver's license and a gas bill to confirm my address. Thank you very much for your help.

Sincerely,

Broke D. Joe

TRW Credit Report Sample

This is your TRW consumer identification number. Please refer to this number when you call or write TRW.

Broke Joe
Nowhere Lane
Debt City. Any State 00000

HOW TO READ THIS REPORT:

AN EXPLANATORY ENCLOSURE ACCOMPANIES THIS REPORT. IT DESCRIBES YOUR CREDIT RIGHTS AND OTHER HELPFUL INFORMATION. IF THE ENCLOSURE IS MISSING. OR YOU HAVE QUESTIONS ABOUT THIS REPORT. PLEASE CONTACT THE OFFICE LISTED ON THE LAST PAGE.

YOUR CREDIT HISTORY

THIS INFORMATION COMES FROM PUBLIC RECORDS OR ORGANIZATIONS THAT HAVE GRANTED CREDIT TO YOU. AN ASTERISK BY AN ACCOUNT INDICATES THAT THIS ITEM MAY REQUIRE FURTHER REVIEW BY A PROSPECTIVE CREDITOR WHEN CHECKING YOUR CREDIT HISTORY. IF YOU BELIEVE ANY OF THE INFORMATION IS INCORRECT PLEASE LET US KNOW

ACCOUNT   DESCRIPTION

1 AMERICAN EXPRESS OPTIMA   THIS CREDIT CARD ACCOUNT WAS OPENED 5/1/90 AND
P O BOX 7871/SROC   HAS REVOLVING REPAYMENT TERMS. YOU HAVE
FORT LAUDERDALE FL 33329   CONTRACTUAL RESPONSIBILITY FOR THIS ACCOUNT
ACCT   #   AND ARE PRIMARILY RESPONSIBLE FOR ITS PAYMENT
CREDIT LIMIT : $4,800.

AS OF 5/1/90. THIS OPEN ACCOUNT IS CURRENT AND ALL PAYMENTS ARE BEING MADE ON TIME. BALANCE $2,500 ON 7/3/96. MONTHS REVIEWED: 75

2 CHASE MANHATTAN BANK   THIS CREDIT CARD ACCOUNT WAS OPENED 3/1/95 AND
802 DELAWARE AVENUE   HAS REVOLVING REPAYMENT TERMS. YOU HAVE
WILMINGTON DE 19801   CONTRACTUAL RESPONSIBILITY FOR THIS ACCOUNT
ACCT   #   AND ARE PRIMARILY RESPONSIBLE FOR ITS PAYMENT
CREDIT LIMIT : $9,000.

AS OF 7/1/96. THIS OPEN ACCOUNT IS CURRENT AND ALL PAYMENTS ARE BEING MADE ON TIME. BALANCE $0 ON 7/5/96. MONTHS REVIEWED: 17

PLEASE HELP US HELP YOU:

AT TRW WE KNOW HOW IMPORTANT YOUR GOOD CREDIT IS TO YOU. IT IS EQUALLY IMPORTANT TO US THAT OUR INFORMATION BE ACCURATE AND UP TO DATE. LISTED BELOW IS THE INFORMATION YOU GAVE US WHEN YOU ASKED FOR THIS REPORT. IF THE INFORMATION IS NOT CORRECT OR YOU DID NOT SUPPLY US WITH FULL NAME. ADDRESS FOR THE PAST FIVE YEARS. SOCIAL SECURITY NUMBER AND YEAR OF BIRTH. THIS REPORT MAY NOT BE COMPLETE. IF THIS INFORMATION IS INCOMPLETE OR NOT ACCURATE. PLEASE LET US KNOW

YOUR NAME   BROKE JOE   SOCIAL SECURITY# 000-00-0000

ADDRESS   NOWHERE LANE   YEAR OF BIRTH 1975
DEBT CITY. ANY STATE 00000

COMPLIMENTARY CREDIT REPORT (CCR) P-821304000   8/3/96 08:05:18 PAGE 1

13

3

ESTABLISH GOOD CREDIT

Penny Tip:

*Responsible behavior will
afford you great rewards.*

Very rarely is any individual void of credit altogether. Your credit rating may be bad but if you have one personal utility bill, there is still someone willing to advance you service for a deferred payment. For instance, you don't pay the electric bill for a month in advance before you can turn on your lights at home. You are generally allowed to use your utilities first and pay later. This is a form of credit that most people do not acknowledge. 'Utilities Credit' is actually the most basic form of credit that is generally extended to everyone irrespective of financial standing. Unlike applying for Visa or MasterCard credit, 'utilities credit' does not consider your annual income and monthly expenses as a determining factor for credit approval.

Let's face it, Mr. NY Bell could care less if you live in a $3 storage box with monthly expenses of $5000, as long as he can throw some wire on a pole and give you a telephone line. The only prerequisite is your name, social security number, and in few cases a minimal deposit for installation charges provided you have no previous delinquent account or unpaid balances. Albeit utilities creditors are less stringent about financial standing, they too want assurance that you will pay for the services used.

So when you have had bad credit in the past, your utilities become a vehicle to establish good credit. Of course, it is an avenue seldom used. Pay your utility bills on time because sometimes creditors look at your utility bill

17

payments to determine a payment pattern. Also, by doing this you establish good credit with that particular utility, and you allow yourself the opportunity for future perks and discounts when they become available.

At this stage in the game, don't look to apply for credit cards. Your goal is not to persuade a financial institution to give you a credit card. In fact at this point, credit cards will not help you. Often times, it is a credit card that gets you in deep trouble. The way to establish good credit is the old fashioned way; honor your word. Do what you said you would do. Pay every bill on or before the due date. Don't let the company send you second, third, and final notices. It's tacky. Some companies don't keep track of payment reminders, but most do. And in the event that they have to do so, they will make an internal note on your records.

Frankly, if you cannot pay your bills on time, you will never establish good credit. A credit card will only sink you deeper in debt. Keep in mind that credit is trust, which has to be earned. The only way you can earn trust is through a pattern of good behavior. Don't worry about asking for credit card at this point. **Your good behavior will earn you that privilege.**

To attain a good credit rating, you must establish good business relationships with creditors. First, pay your bills on time. Second, open a savings account in which you will save a fixed amount on a monthly basis. This is explained in greater detail later. If the thought that just crossed your mind is, "I can't afford to save now...maybe in the future," continue reading. You will dispel this thought after you read the chapters: Structure Your Savings and Budget with "Elbow Space."

4

MANAGE YOUR EXISTING CREDIT

Penny Tip:

*Take from Peter to pay Paul,
only if it's going to advance
your financial position!*

Maybe your credit is not bad, and all it needs is a face-lift. You may have few credit cards; and you've probably charged a lot on them. Now you're trying to figure out how to pay them off. If this is your case, I suggest that you consolidate your debt to the card with the lowest interest rate. If you have a lot of cards, you may have to consolidate down to two or three cards. The point is that you do not want to pay astronomical finance charges, which hinder you from paying them off quicker.

When you consolidate, it is easier to make larger payments to one credit institution. Instead of sending payments to many different credit card companies, you can narrow it down to one or two companies. This is to your advantage in the long run because you won't end up paying the interest charge on each card. I know this seems elementary, but you'd be surprised how many people are not making ends meet because of this very elementary fact. The key of successful money management is knowing when and how to implement the very basic fundamentals. Consolidate. Again, you can do this your self. Contact the credit card companies to which you would like to transfer other balances, and ask them to send you the proper transfer forms.

Most people know how to take from Peter to pay Paul, but they do it out of pressure to pay on a due date, not necessarily to lower their debt. **There's nothing wrong with taking from Peter to pay Paul, if in doing so**

Paul offers you an attractive deal that will reduce your debt with Peter. This is a strategy that most credit card institutions allow its members.

Actually if you think about it, that's an excellent financial strategy. The problem is that most people use this strategy just to temporarily get creditors off their backs, rather than better their financial position. So they end up in worse condition than when they started off. Unfortunately, that is not proper management. That is finagling! It is important that you plan your financial strategies and use available resources to better your financial condition, not just to beat a deadline, 'to get by'. That's just as bad as going to school to fall asleep in class. When you wake up, you don't know anymore than you did before you went to class, and often times you can't even remember what you thought you knew. Sure, you were there, but it is of no benefit to you whatsoever. You must plan in advance all payments so that you don't end up throwing money away. Allow me to illustrate a real situation. An individual has six credit cards:

Credit Cards	**Interest**	**Limit**
Am ExpOptima	7.9%	$ 4,800
Chase Visa	5.9%	$ 15,000
Citibank Visa	15.9%	$ 5,000
CitibankMasterCard	15.9%	$ 6,100
Bank of America Visa	15.6%	$ 4,400
Wells Fargo Visa	17.9%	$ 1,000

24

Scenario 1

He has a balance on each credit card for which he is paying annual fees.

	Balance	Yr. Fee
Am ExpOptima	$ 963.28	$ 76.10
Chase Visa	$ 2,311.33	$ 136.37
Citibank Visa	$ 4,800.00	$ 763.20
Citibank MasterCard	$ 4,300.00	$ 683.70
Bank of America Visa	$ 3,900.00	$ 608.40
Wells Fargo Visa	$ 218.51	$ 39.11
Totals	**$16,493.12**	**$2,306.88**

Notice, the fees account for 13.99% of the total debt:

$$\frac{\$\,2,306.88}{\$16,493.12} = 13.99\%$$

That's a lot of money especially when there's a cheaper alternative. The problem with scenario 1 is a serious one. This person has most of his debt locked in the higher interest rate credit cards. At the end of the year, he's paying a whopping $2,306.88 just in fees. Because so much money is going towards interest, his debt will be with him for longer. And 'catch 22' is that the longer he has this debt, the more interest he will pay. He will find

25

himself paying interest on unpaid interest. This is called **compound interest**. Avoiding compound interest is sometimes difficult, and that's why shopping for low interest rates becomes of utmost significance. Let us look at a better alternative.

First, arrange all your credit cards by interest rate from lowest to highest.

	Balance	Int.	Limit
Chase Visa	$ 2,311.33	5.9%	$15,000
AmExp Opt	$ 963.28	7.9%	$ 4,800
B of A Visa	$ 3,900.00	15.6%	$ 4,400
Citibank Visa	$ 4,800.00	15.9%	$ 5,000
Citibank MC	$ 4,300.00	15.9%	$ 6,100
W F Visa	$ 218.51	17.9%	$ 1,000

Transfer balances to the lower interest rate cards. Be very careful to stay within your limit when transferring any balances. Remember your existing balances on the cards to which you will transfer so that you do not exceed the limit balances. If you have difficulty remembering the limits on your credit cards, write it down. Do not get in the habit of using credit cards, writing checks, or engaging in any financial transactions without knowing actual limits and balances. If you know that you have made additional charges on your credit card since the last statement, and you're not sure of the existing balance, call the credit card company. They usually reflect up-to-date balances.

On the Chase Visa Card*, you have an available credit of $12,688.67. So transfer the greater balances with the higher interests to the lower cards. Transfer the following balances to the Chase Visa Card at 5.9%:

Bank of America Visa	$ 3 500.00
Citibank Visa	$ 4 800.00
Citibank MasterCard	$ 4 300.00

*This card has a limit of $15,000 with an existing balance of $2311.33

On the AmExp Optima*, you have an available credit of $3,836.72. Transfer the following balances to the AmExp Optima Card at 7.9%:

Bank of America Visa	$ 400.00
Wells Fargo Visa	$ 218.51

*This card has a limit of $4,800 with an existing balance of $963.28

27

Now let's see a much improved scenario.

Scenario 2

He has transferred all his debt to the lower interest credit cards.

	Balance	Yr. Fee
Am Exp. Optima	$ 1,581.79	$ 124.97
Chase Visa	$14,911.33	$ 879.77
Totals	**$16,493.12**	**$1,004.74**

Now, the fees account for 6.09% of the total debt instead of 13.99%.

Your Scenario

List your credit cards, <u>limit</u>, and interest.

Credit Card   Limit   Interest

1)_____ _____   _____

2)_____ _____   _____

3)_____ _____   _____

4)_____ _____   _____

List your credit cards, <u>debt</u>, and interest.

Credit Card   Debt   Interest

1)_____ _____   _____

2)_____ _____   _____

3)_____ _____   _____

4)_____ _____   _____

Do you notice the difference between scenario 1 and 2? There is a savings amount of $1,302.14. Why pay interest on this money when you can earn interest for it at your bank. This person has not only saved money, but has paid off four credit cards in one shot. This will reflect positively on his credit rating.

In retrospect, one would say it almost seems foolish that he didn't bother to charge most of his purchases on the Chase initially. Well, it turns out that at the time of his purchase, the Chase limit was only $8,000.00 and it did not approve such large charges at once. Only Bank of America, Citibank Visa, and MasterCard approved him for such large amounts. But the job of a money manager is never done. It is his responsibility to keep track of his credit card limit increases and interest rate changes. How well he fulfills his responsibilities as a money manager is what will make the difference between financial freedom and economic enslavement.

Thus, as a money manager, based on the purchases, you must determine when to use credit cards, checks, or cash. That brings me to my next point. Whenever you are making a large purchase, such as a car, you may want to consider making the purchase with a credit card check. Most credit cards offer checks. You just have to request them. Of course, never forget to consider your available limit and interest rate. If your credit card interest rate is lower than that of the auto dealer's financing, use your credit card. Finance your own purchase. There is a great advantage to using a credit card. The bank doesn't take a lien position on your property. Should you default with your credit cards, your property will not be repossessed. Of course even with such advantages, you don't want to ever default because it will ruin your credit rating. But just be mindful that when you use the auto dealer's financing and you default with them, not only do you lose your property to the 'Repo Man', but you then have a judgment for the unpaid balance, and it ruins your credit rating. A triple whammy!

Of course, we never want to default under any circumstances, but we must always plan for the possibility of unforeseen adverse circumstances. In doing so, we must weigh the advantages and the disadvantages of each plan of action in the event that the plan does not materialize. Minimize your loss!

31

5

STRUCTURE YOUR SAVINGS

Penny Tip:

If you won't pay yourself for what you do,
why should anyone else?

Open a checking and savings account at a bank of your choice, if you haven't already done so. Your checking account will become what we call your 'payment processing center' (PPC). Every two weeks PPC will be responsible for paying all bills, creditors, vendors, etc... It is very important that at this stage PPC only processes payments every two weeks. This will control the amount of money that leaves PPC - your pocket. In the budget stage we will discuss what payments are acceptable to be processed by PPC.

Find out at your job whether or not direct deposit of your paycheck is an option. If it is, arrange to have your paychecks directly deposited to your checking account. This way your paychecks are deposited automatically, and there is no opportunity for you to spend any of it outside of PPC guidelines. Should you have any other types of income such as investment interests, child support, etc...arrange for direct deposit if possible.

If direct deposit is not available to you, do not get discouraged. This simply means that you will have to exercise a little more will power and discipline than those with direct deposit. Every payday, you will have to deposit your own checks. You may not take any cash back under any circumstances.

You will then include yourself as one of the vendors, which PPC will pay monthly. **As a hard working**

employee, you provide a service for the upkeep and management of your household. And for this, you must get compensated. If you hire someone to help you with your finances, taxes, and money management issues, they would instantly become one of your vendors that PPC would have to pay. Then why can you not pay yourself, if you provide your household with the same service? It is extremely important that you begin to structure your household finances as that of a business. Make arrangements with your bank to have a monthly automatic transfer from your checking to your savings. We will discuss your fee, the fixed amount for automatic transfer, later in the budget stage.

Moreover, the bank gets a clear view of your financial activity. This allows them to evaluate your ability to meet certain financial obligations. Writing checks within your means, and building a savings account simultaneously is definitely something that banks encourage. Remember that our goal is to establish good credit. Once you have established a pattern of good money management that the bank can identify, the likelihood that your bank will offer you a credit card is great.

Saving a fixed amount on a monthly basis, is the best way to prove to a financial institution that you have a pattern of good behavior in terms of finance. It clearly communicates that if you can save $30 to $50 a month, you can certainly make minimum monthly payments of

$15 to $20 to a credit card. The rationale is quite simple. Banks and/or institutions with great financial solvency back credit cards. If you establish a good business relationship with Chase Manhattan, guess who is going to extend you a pre-approved credit line. That's right. Chase Manhattan will be the first to offer you your first Visa or Mastercard credit card. And you will have reached your goal, a financial institution that trusts you.

6

BUDGET WITH "ELBOW SPACE"

Penny Tip:

Buy the shrimp dinner,
only it costs less than your
income minus expenses.

The budget stage is the turning point for your credit clean up. Forget about your old set plans and pre-existing budgets. Here and now you will develop a new budget and time line that you will follow. First, list your net income, which is the amount of money you take home after paying taxes. Then list all of your expenses. This is where we separate the bare necessities from the waste "wants." Whenever you have a debt to service, you automatically forfeit your rights to spend on "wants" first. **Debts are paid first and "wants" last.**

The concept is also quite simple. As long as you owe someone for services rendered, you may not spend their money. While movies, theater, ballet, eat out dinners, amusement parks, etc... may be uplifting and fulfilling, they are not 'bare bone' necessities. In all fairness, if someone owed you three thousand dollars, you wouldn't really want to hear that he just bought himself a beautiful gift to wear to a Broadway show. I guarantee, you will not be the least bit empathetic with him regarding his proclaimed financial distress.

Your budget should be as lean as possible. Whatever is not absolute necessity should be cut off. I'm not suggesting that you revert to a primitive standard of living, having crackers for dinner and saving the box to make cardboard shoes. You don't have to live in deprivation. By all means, buy the shrimp dinner. And do buy yourself a decent pair of shoes that will hold up on a rainy day.

41

What I'm simply saying is that you must prioritize to service the debts before purchasing "wants." And you will determine this by listing all your debt items, income sources, and monthly expenses. Use the following pages.

DEBTS TO SERVICE

List all your current and past due debt (including credit cards)

Creditor	Balance Due
1. _____	$_____
2. _____	$_____
3. _____	$_____
4. _____	$_____
5. _____	$_____
6. _____	$_____
7. _____	$_____
8. _____	$_____
9. _____	$_____
10. _____	$_____
Total Debt	$_____

INCOME (Please list)

Net Wages $_____

Child Support $_____

Interests $_____

Capital Gains $_____

Other income $_____

Total $_____

These are your resources from which you will allocate to pay any pre-existing debts and obligations. Since your funds are limited, it is crucial that you do not squander any.

EXPENSES

List all your monthly expenses.

Rent/Mortgage	$_____
Telephone	$_____
Gas/Electric	$_____
Food/Toiletries	$_____
Auto/Transportation	$_____
Medical Insurance	$_____
Child Care	$_____
Education (books/tuition)	$_____
Savings	$_____
Debts (page 11)	$_____
Total	$_____

Expense Percentage Allocation

Expense percentage allocation will no doubt vary from household to household. You may have other important expenses, not listed here. If so, include such expenses into your expense allocation percentage guide. This guide will give you a good view of your financial landscape, and help you keep track of your spending.

A percentage of your total monthly income should be allocated to each monthly expense. The following is a list of monthly expense allocation.

Rent/Mortgage	30%
Telephone	3%
Utilities	12%
Food	10%
Auto/trans.	13%
Savings***	10%
Debts***	15%
Misc.	7%

*** As long as there is a debt to service, at least 15% of net income should be allotted to paying off that debt. When that debt is paid, that percentage of income should go towards savings. The main goal is to increase savings to a maximum degree. Therefore, the savings percentage will fluctuate upwards but should never go below 10% of net income.

Tithing Households

If you are of the Judeo-Christian faith that requires you to tithe 10% of your income to your church or religious establishment, by all means include it as a necessary expense on your list. Since tithes are 10% of your income, the percentage allotment will vary in other areas. You may decide to take from your savings, provided that they do not go below 10%. If your savings are not enough to cover your tithes, use the miscellaneous percentage allotment and/or readjust other items.

For many people the religious practice of tithing is of utmost importance, and needs to be accounted for in the household's financial structure.

The following percentage allocation is appropriate for the tithing household.

Tithes	10%
Rent/Mortgage	30%
Telephone	3%
Utilities	10%
Food	10%
Auto/trans.	10%
Savings	10%
Debts	10%
Misc.	7%

Now that you have already listed all of your debt, income and expenses, make the percentage calculations for each expense category.

Follow the example below. If you bring home $2000.00 every month, the following guide applies.

Net Income		**$**	**2,000.00**
Rent/Mrtg.	($2000x.30)	$	600.00
Telephone	($2000x.03)	$	60.00
Utilities	($2000x.12)	$	240.00
Food	($2000x.10)	$	200.00
Auto/trans.	($2000x.13)	$	260.00
Savings	($2000x.10)	$	200.00
Debts	($2000x.15)	$	300.00
Misc.	($2000x.07)	$	140.00

Once you have figured out the dollar amount for each expense based on a percentage of your income, with the exception of savings and debt payments, none of the other expenses should exceed the dollar amount allotment. While the expense payments should not exceed the allotement, the debt payments and savings shall not fall below the percentage allotment. In fact, you should seek to increase debt payments and savings if your resources allow you to.

48

Fill in **your figures** in the blank spaces provided below.

		Old Method	**New Method**
Net Income		$_____	$_____
Rent/Mrtg.	(30%)	$_____	$_____
Telephone	(3%)	$_____	$_____
Utilities	(12%)	$_____	$_____
Food	(10%)	$_____	$_____
Auto/Trans	(13%)	$_____	$_____
Savings	(10%)	$_____	$_____
Debts	(15%)	$_____	$_____
Misc.	(7%)	$_____	$_____
(a)_____		$_____	$_____
(b)_____		$_____	$_____
(c)_____		$_____	$_____
(d)_____		$_____	$_____

As I stated earlier, you may have more or less expenses. In the event that you have an additional expense, you will meet that obligation with the Miscellaneous 7%. If you do not have any additional expenses, the Miscellaneous allotment should go toward the debt. This will allow you to pay off your debt quicker. After you have done so, the Miscellaneous should then be added to Savings.

You may always increase the debt percentage allotment to pay off debt by borrowing from the savings and/or miscellaneous, provided the savings percentage never goes below 10%. This is your new guide, and these are the only expenses that PPC should pay!

Let's go back, remember the checking and savings accounts that you set up at the bank? And your monthly fee for your services? Well now is the time to have your PPC checking account automatic transfer the monthly savings amount indicated on your guide, better known as your fee that we discussed earlier, to your savings account. Your monthly fee is the amount you will deposit into your savings. Once in place, your savings will begin without your having to lift a finger.

You must follow your guide. Once you have set a budget figure within your percentage allowance, you should not go beyond that figure.

Time-line Budgets

Should you have specific financial goals and a time frame within which to accomplish such goals, you need to construct a time-line budget. The time-line budget is a more structured budget designed to help you better monitor your financial course in relation to time. It allows you to itemized every expense detail, income source, debt balance on a bi-weekly or monthly basis for a projected time frame.

50

Whereupon you decide to purchase a brand new Dell 450Mhz II Pentium with MMX computer, for instance, you must determine the following particulars:

- Cost of the purchase
- Fees and hidden charges in relation to the purchase, if any
- Time frame within which you intend to purchase
- Your disposable income for the purchase
- Other available monetary resources, if necessary

After you've considered the aforementioned, you will draft your time-line budget. This is the blueprint on which you will pencil out all the financial details of your income, expenses, and the proposed purchase within your projected time frame. The time-line budget will allow you to determine, with a great degree of accuracy, whether or not your purchase is feasible within the projected time period. You may have to create several time-line budgets before deciding upon one.

Likening this experience to that of an architect drafting a floor plan for a house, the first draft is seldom the final blueprint. Therefore, don't get discouraged if your time-line budget seems impractical. Go back to the drawing board and do it again. You may have to change your projected time frame, increase your savings, or decide upon a less expensive purchase. Let's pencil out a time-line budget, considering the following particulars.

51

Monthly Net income:	$ 2,000.00
Price of intended purchase:	$ 2,500.00
Existing debt:	$ 2,000.00
Monthly Expenses:	$ 1,500.00
Monthly Savings (10%):	$ 200.00

Since there is an existing debt, you must prioritize your budget in this order: existing debt, monthly expenses, then the computer purchase. Therefore, $300.00 (15% of $2,000.00) will be allotted towards the existing debt on a monthly basis until it's completely paid off. From the remaining balance, $1,500.00 is allotted to the monthly expenses, leaving $200.00 to allot towards your intended purchase. Of course, should your monthly expenses decrease from time to time, you may appropriate the difference towards your intended purchase.

So considering these specifics, your time-line will look something like the following. Although this is a monthly time-line budget, you may construct a biweekly time-line budget, detailing your expenditure and/or cash disbursement for each pay period.

TIME-LINE
(FIVE MONTHS)

	Jan	Feb	Mar	Apr	May	YTD
Rent	$725	$725	$725	$725	$725	**$3,625**
Tithes	$200	$200	$200	$200	$200	**$1,000**
Savings (10%)	$200	$200	$200	$200	$200	**$1,000**
Light & Gas	$50	$50	$50	$50	$50	**$250**
Car Insurance	$150	$150	$150	$150	$150	**$750**
Phone/Pager	$50	$50	$50	$50	$50	**$250**
Groceries	$100	$100	$100	$100	$100	**$500**
Car Gas	$25	$25	$25	$25	$25	**$125**
Debt: $2000	$300	$300	$300	$300	$300	**$1,500**
Purchase: Computer	$200	$200	$200	$200	$200	**$1,000**
Total Expenses	$2,000	$2,000	$2,000	$2,000	$2,000	**$10,000**
Checking Account	$0	$0	$0	$0	$0	**$0**
Savings Account	$200	$400	$600	$800	$1,000	**$1,000**

Assuming you are a tither of the Judeo-Christian faith, in five months time, you will have paid off 75% ($1,500) of your existing debt, and saved 40% ($1000.00) for your computer. If you are of a non Judeo-Christian faith, and tithing is not required of you, you will have paid off 75% ($1,500) of your existing debt, and saved 80% ($2000.00) for your computer.

Clearly, the time-line budget allows you to realistically itemize your expenses and/or cash disbursements in relation to time with a great degree of accuracy.

7

BUDGET FOR THE "STILL AT HOMERS"

Penny Tips

Save NOW!

While the principle of budgeting does not change, the approach often does. The budgeting habits of people who do not have financial obligations are quite different from those who do. Individuals who live with parents, or in households in which someone else covers all expenses, have less financial concerns and pressures for the most part. These people are in the best position to save a fortune. Maybe their only expenses are a phone bill and a few school supplies.

If this happens to be your ideal reality, the following percentage expense allocation is for you.

Food	10%
Auto/trans.	13%
Debts	15%
Misc.	3%
Savings	55%

As already stated, your case may vary much more or less, but the above percentage allocation serves as a guide to keep you focused. Rent, utilities, phone, and food are expenses that usually constitute 55% of an average monthly income. On the premise that these are paid expenses in your household, you would automatically add 55% to the 10% you are already saving. But assuming that you have a phone bill, and transportation expenses to cover, your savings percentage will be 55% as opposed to 65%. The logic behind this is that under any other

57

circumstances you would have to pay these expenses regardless of any other financial obligations.

Fill in **your figures** in the blank spaces provided below.

		Old Method	**New Method**
Net Income		$_____	$ **Same**
Food	(10%)	$_____	$_____
Auto/Trans.	(13%)	$_____	$_____
Debts	(15%)	$_____	$_____
Savings	(55%)	$_____	$_____
Misc.	(3%)	$_____	$_____
(a)_____		$_____	$_____
(b)_____		$_____	$_____
(c)_____		$_____	$_____
(d)_____		$_____	$_____

You will be saving 55% of your net income. It's that simple! Again, if you happen to be living at home and paying for some of the utilities, you may deduct that percentage from your savings. Do not spend money unnecessarily. Living will never be this cheap when you move out on your own. **Save, Save, Save!**

Let's explore a hypothetical situation. Suppose you are a student, who works a part-time job, and lives at home with parents. Your schedule only allows you to work 20 to 25 hours a week. On a monthly basis, you bring home $640.00. "Who can live on that?" The 'still at homers', and at a great advantage.

Remember, we have already established that you don't carry the full financial burden, as do those who live on their own. Therefore, your ability to save is more than feasible. Only at this point in your life will you have a head start that will keep you in financial lead by the time you move out on your own. Take this opportunity and do not dismiss it with, "I have plenty of time" or "I'll start my savings plan when I get on my own." No. Start now.

If your particulars are as follow:

Monthly Net income:	$ 640.00
Monthly Savings (55%):	$ 352.00
Monthly Expenses:	$ 288.00

Tithes:	$ 64.00
Trans.:	$ 80.00
Phone/Pager:	$ 50.00
Snacks	$ 64.00
Entertainment/Misc.:	$ 30.00

Your time-line budget should look like this:

TIME-LINE
(FIVE MONTHS)

	Jan	Feb	Mar	Apr	May	YTD
Rent	$0	$0	$0	$0	$0	$0
Tithes	$64	$64	$64	$64	$64	$320
Savings (55%)	$352	$352	$352	$352	$352	$1,760
Light & Gas	$0	$0	$0	$0	$0	$0
Transp./Gas	$80	$80	$80	$80	$80	$400
Phone/Pager	$50	$50	$50	$50	$50	$250
Snacks	$64	$64	$64	$64	$64	$320
Entertainment/ Misc.	$30	$30	$30	$30	$30	$150
Total Expenses	$640	$640	$640	$640	$640	$3,200
Checking Account	$0	$0	$0	$0	$0	$0
Savings Account	$352	$352	$352	$352	$352	$1,760

8

SAFEGUARD AGAINST BOUNCING CHECKS

Penny Tip:

Sort and process twice a month,
and keep a running balance.

Are you like millions of Americans who do not bother to adjust the checkbook balance every time a check is written or a debit is authorized in their accounts? Do you frequently misjudge your actual bank balance, and end up bouncing lots of checks? Bad! This is a very bad habit but don't worry. You're still not a "lost case". There is a plan of action that will help you change this ill practice. Once you implement this record-keeping system, you will never miscalculate your account balances and/or bounce a check ever again. This is more than a promise; it's a fact.

Take a look at and practice with the bills that PPC receives and must pay for **HOUSEHOLD 1.**

HOUSEHOLD 1	EXPENSES	DUE DATES
Rent/Mrtg.	$ 550.00	1^{st}(next month)
Telephone	$ 52.03	7^{th}(next month)
Utilities Gas	$ 12.01	12^{th}(next month)
Utilities Electric	$ 61.08	18th
Food	$ 178.00	1st, 15th
Auto/trans.	$ 270.59	3^{rd}(next month)
Savings	$ 235.00	15th
Chase Credit Card	$1,100.00	21st

From now on, you will only process bills twice a month. For most people paydays are usually on the 15th and 30th. If you get paid biweekly, you will process your bills on your paydays. This will help you better monitor the checks you write.

Whenever you receive bills in the mail, sort them according to due dates. Make a 15th and a 30th pile. All bills that are due after the 15th but before the 30th, you will put in the 15th pile. Those bills due after the 30th, but before the 15th of the following month, you will put in the 30th pile (see calendar on page 66).

For example, take a look at **HOUSEHOLD 1.** Rent is due on the 1st; phone due on the 7th; electricity due on the 18th; gas due on the 12th; car note due on the 3rd; bank charge on the 16th; credit card due on the 21st; and savings due on the 15th (automatic transfer date to be arranged with your bank.) Pay close attention due date. Determine whether the due date indicated on the bill pertains to the current month or the next month. For instance, assuming we are in the month of March, the rent due date of the 1st pertains to the month of April. Therefore, it would be paid on the 30th of March, before the 1st of April.

This sorting system is designed to allow you to always process your bills within the due dates, and not after. This way you are certain to not incur late fees, and/or ruin any business relations.

64

Let's sort the bills that are to be processed for
HOUSEHOLD 1:

These bills are to be processed and paid on **the 15th** of
current month:

Credit card	21st
Electricity	18th
Savings	15th
Bank charge	16th

These bills are to be processed and paid on **the 30th** of
current month:

Car note	3rd	(NEXT MONTH)
Rent	1st	(NEXT MONTH)
Phone	7th	(NEXT MONTH)
Gas	12th	(NEXT MONTH)

**All bills must be processed for payment on or before
the PPC processing date prior to the bills' due dates.**

MARCH 1998

SUN	MON	TUE	WED	THU	FRI	SAT
1	2	3	4	5	6	7
8	9	10	11	12	13	14
15 **Payday(1)** Savings-1	16 Bank charge-1	17	18 Electric Bill-1	19	20	21 Credit Card-1
22	23	24	25	26	27	28
29	30 **Payday(2)**	31				

APRIL 1998

SUN	MON	TUE	WED	THU	FRI	SAT
			1 Rent-2	2	3 Car note Bill-1	4
5	6	7 Phone Bill-2	8	9	10	11
12 Gas Bill-2	13	14	15 **Payday** Savings	16	17	18
19	20	21	22	23	24	25
26	27	28	29	30 **Payday**		

March 15th paycheck pays for the savings, bank charge, electric, and credit card bills; and **March 30**[th] paycheck pays for rent, car note, phone, and gas bills. Notice that all bills are processed on or before their due dates. The credit card bill, for example, although is not due until the 21st of the month, must be processed on the 15th because that is the processing date prior to the bill's due date. Had the bill been processed on the 30th of that month, instead of the 15th, the bill would have been paid after the due date of the 21st, and possibly incurred late fees. So, with this procedure, **HOUSEHOLD 1** will never be late with its bills.

Once you have sorted your bills according to the processing dates, you will write out the payments in your checkbook, and immediately adjust the balance to reflect the payment of the bill. Do this with all the bills as they come in. You may assign a check number to each payment in your checkbook, and even fill out the check. Write the assigned check number on the bill and keep it in a file for your records. **DO NOT** sign the check until the actual funds are deposited in your account. **You are merely processing and recording transactions to keep an accurate and updated checkbook balance.** This will let you know at all times how much money PPC has available for check processing.

Each bill has been sorted for payment within its due date. The bills that have due dates after the 30th of the previous month and before the 15th of the current month, such as the gas bill, are processed with the 30th of the previous month. This is extremely important. This means that you will have to prepay this bill on the 30th of the previous month, not the 15th of the current month, after the due date of the bill.

Allow me to show you...

PPC

Chk #	Date	Description	Debit	Credit	Balance
					$444.39
Trnsfr	3/15	Savings transfer	235.00		$209.39
801	3/15	Dept. of Power Electric	61.08		$148.31
SrvChg	3/15	Bank Charge	7.00		$141.31
802	3/15	Good Food Grocery Store	178.00		($36.69)
803	3/15	Chase Visa	1,100.00		($1,136.69)
Dep	3/15	Direct Deposit Paycheck		1,148.15	$ 11.46
804	3/30	Toyota Motor Car - Note	270.59		($259.13)
805	3/30	Affordable Housing - Rent	550.00		($809.13)
806	3/30	US Phone Bell	52.03		($861.16)
807	3/30	Gas Company	12.01		($873.17)
808	3/30	Chase Visa - 2nd Pymt	260.00		($1,133.17)
Dep	3/30	Direct Deposit Paycheck		1,148.15	$ 14.98

Note:

Throughout the month, your running balances are mostly negatives amounts. But as long as the negative balance amount never goes below ($1,148.15), which is the amount that your net income can cover every pay period, you are fine. Since your net income per pay period of $1,148.15 is enough to cover the negative amount, PPC will have enough resources to process all transactions for the period. You will always write checks within your means. Should the negative balance go below the ($1,148.15), this is an immediate red flag. Know that you have over-paid somewhere. Go back and scrutinize every transaction. Maybe you have to reduce your savings amount (remember no less than 10% of your monthly income).

Please bear in mind that <u>negative balances reflected in the checkbook may not be actual negative balances at the bank</u>. Certain transactions may not have not been processed at the bank yet. You are merely maintaining these debit figures as a reminder that you have committed these amounts to pay for certain expenses. This way you know at all times how much of your check is already committed and not available to you.

Go back to the previous page. Notice how PPC made a second payment to the Chase Credit Card. After all other bills are paid, the additional funds should be used to pay off pre-existing debts. Reduce your debt fast so that you can focus on saving. If there is no debt, transfer the excess to savings.

Get in the habit of calling your bank's automated system if they have one. Most banks have an 800# automated system. Go over the account activity. This will tell you whether or not your paycheck has posted, checks have been paid, and there are any additional service charges. Even if you think that all is fine, check anyway. The banks are run by human beings like you and I; and they make mistakes. Unfortunately, a mistake doesn't keep a check from bouncing. Also, there may be times when you are simply unaware of legitimate minor charges, what I call "hidden expenses." It is your responsibility, and to your benefit, to make sure that everything is accounted for accurately. Keep in mind that you hired yourself as you're household's money manager. That's what managers do; they oversee everything.

If you implement this sorting and processing system, you will never fall behind on your financial responsibilities. Moreover, after a history evidencing financial responsibility, creditors and vendors will offer you privileges including, but not limited to, extended grace periods, discounts, increased credit limits, and gifts.

9

DISCIPLINE

Penny Tip:

*Define the controls for your
financial landscape;
establish and practice them.*

Until now, you probably have confined yourself to a complacent and comfortable stage between failure and success. And if that is comfortable to you, then nothing I say regarding discipline will prompt you to commit to progress. However, the fact that you are reading this book is a great indication that you are not comfortable. Thus, your discomfort, more so than the words on this page, will compel you to a path of strict financial discipline.

What can I say about discipline that you don't already know or haven't already heard? Nothing. By now, you've probably heard all the 'discipline' speeches ever given. You've heard them from your parents, teachers, tutors, and coaches. "Without discipline, you won't be successful." "You must be disciplined to succeed." "Discipline is the key to every locked door." That's a simple enough concept to grasp. Certainly nobody has any difficulty understanding the relationship between a key and a locked door. It's common knowledge that a key is the tool that opens a locked door. Sometimes these 'discipline lines' are so elementary, you don't know whether to take offense or thank the person who just dropped them on you. Yet the common reaction is a stone-face expression that has "I know that!" written all over it. They sound more like nursery rhymes than words of wisdom. We all know that discipline is the key that opens every locked door. But if you think about, that statement is as vague and abstract as "The Wipensteimer is the soap that cleans every dish." Although you know what soap

73

looks like, you couldn't identify a 'Wipensteimer' if you saw one because a Weipensteimer is not an actual soap, neither is discipline an actual key. Ironically, as elementary as these lines might sound, they envelop a conceptual complexity that keeps you from opening the locked door in front of you.

What is discipline? We have learned all the lines and rhymes, statements and phrases about it. But we don't know what it is. We know countless analogous descriptions of it, but we don't know <u>what</u> <u>defines</u> discipline. So, we get lost in a syntactical play of words. Yet pressed for an answer, we offer "self-control!" Good answer. But again, what does that mean? How would you gauge self-control in your life? How do you know when you're exercising self-control and when you're not? Let's identify discipline.

Discipline is a conscious decision to put a learned control, the enforced order of an environment, into practice to achieve a specific outcome.

74

Consider the controls of the following environments:

Environment:

Government   Corporations   Schools

Controls:

Laws	Policies	Academic
Codes	Procedures	curriculum
Ordinances	Regulation	

Outcome:

Crime-less	Good standing	Degrees
society	with state	Graduation
Rights	Business license	Certification

Government implements laws to achieve a crime-less society. Laws are the controls of government. "Obey the laws and you don't go to jail." But that statement, as simple as it may be, does not tell you how to stay out of jail. Until the laws are defined, the concept of obeying laws remains abstract. For instance, if the law is defined as, "if you steal, you go to jail," then you know what you must not do to obey the law. Otherwise, it remains as vague as a parent telling a child, "be good." If the control to be good has not been defined, the child does not know exactly what he has to do or not do to 'be good'. 'Be good' must be defined with specificity such as, "don't open the door to strangers." And if you have children, you know that you have to constantly define controls within controls and definitions within definitions. 'Be good' means "don't open the door to strangers," and that means, "don't open the door to anyone other than mommy or daddy."

In many ways, we are just like children. We don't process information correctly if it's not specifically defined and broken down to its lowest denominators. The control of discipline must be established, defined and broken to its lowest denominators in order for us to identify, master, and practice it.

Let's get started. From this day on, your financial discipline will be putting the following controls you've learned in the previous chapters into practice.

Environment:

- Your Household Finances

Controls:

- Honor your word at all times
- Always pay your bills (debts) first
- Do not exceed the established amounts in your budget
- Keep a running balance of your checking account (PPC)
- Arrange automatic transfer from PPC to savings with bank
- Save no less than 10% of your monthly income
- Arrange Direct Deposits with your employer (if possible)
- If you have credit cards, use the one with lower interest rate

Outcome:

- Accelerated financial growth
- Excellent credit rating

Of course, everyone's financial landscape is different. The more complex your financial environment becomes, the more controls you will have to implement to your financial discipline. It is your duty to regularly analyze your financial condition to determine what additional controls, if any, are necessary. This is very important because your outcome is contingent upon your controls. If you don't enforce your controls, the outcome (consequences) will reflect just that.

Ten years ago, a neighbor, with the help of his son, started a furniture upholstery business. Everyone in the community got his couch, sofa, or favorite chair reupholstered. Needless to say his business was very successful. In his first year of operation, his company had an 1800% return on his $10,000 start-up investment. And in the second year, the profits doubled. Soon after, he bought a house. Basking in the newfound fortune, his son dropped out of college to go full-time into the upholstery business. Six years later, Uncle Sam put a lien on his house and all his upholstered furniture for not paying taxes.

"First of all, I'm self employed now. Secondly, I moved and they (IRS representatives) never sent me the tax forms in the mail." Although it's common knowledge that tax forms can be obtained practically anywhere, such as post offices and libraries, that was one of the several reasons he gave for not filing his taxes. But when "they" made it clear to him that he has a legal responsibility to file his taxes whether or not he moves or receives tax forms in the mail, he immediately intimated to the IRS representative that, "the system is screwed up. The tax payers should be kept informed."

Notice, he took the blame from "they" and tossed it on "the system." Blame never starts with "me" or "I." It always lies somewhere between "they" and "the system." Never once did it occur to him that perhaps he should have done his research as it relates to his changing financial landscape. No one knows his financial situation better than he does. Having been an employee for the better part of his life, his duty was to canvass regulatory agencies and inquire about the legal and financial responsibilities of Employers and self-employed individuals in order to implement the proper controls for his business and household.

Not only was that a public humiliation, but a very costly experience. Today his declaration is "I'll never do that again. I've learned from my mistake." Who wouldn't? Considering the painfully defeating feeling of watching someone drive up to your home of many years and haul away all your valuables along with the cat in broaddaylight, while onlookers murmur and snicker, is an experience that becomes indelibly impressed in anyone's mind. Any mistake that generates such an experience is not one to be easily forgotten. Unfortunately, those are usually the only mistakes from which we learn - the mistakes that generate personal experiences.

How many times have you said, "I learn from my mistakes!" Countless times. And for all practical purposes, we all would like to believe that we do. But that is not the truth. More often than not, our mistakes lead to experiences that play out in other people's lives. If I told you that the last time you bounced a $50.00 check, a college student in his senior year was kicked out of school, and you're the reason he didn't graduate; you'd probably say "that's ridiculous."

Yet examine the sequence of events, cause and effect, and you'll realize that it's not so ridiculous at all. People are adversely affected, with sometimes devastating consequences, by "little mistakes." For example, a student working part-time at a local grocery store, rushes to the bank on payday to deposit her paycheck. She then runs to her landlord to pay her rent that was due two days ago. Three days later, the bank notifies her of a returned check for non-sufficient funds. The check she gave her landlord bounced. It turns out that her employer was not able to cover payroll because some customer checks he received did not clear at the bank. And your fifty-dollar check was among the customer checks that bounced. Although the landlord accepted her apology and understood that these were circumstances beyond her control, the hard-working student was evicted. Shortly after, she was laid off and standing on the unemployment line. She could no longer afford her apartment, tuition and books. Other people's "little mistakes," got her kicked out of her apartment and school. All her efforts went 'down the tubes.'

"Her employer couldn't cover $50.00?" Sure he could cover $50.00. Unfortunately, that figure turned into $1500.00 when 20 other customers made the same "little mistake." He couldn't cover her $1500.00 salary in addition to his monthly expenses. In the meantime, each customer is saying, "Well, I only bounced one small check. My check wasn't the reason his business went under, and she lost her job, schooling, and apartment."

The human character is inherently flawed with "irresponsibility" and "blame displacement." These are conditions that must undergo lifetime treatment with substantial dosage of "Discipline." Therefore, let us treat our conditions so that we can live functional lives. It's worth noting that individuals without discipline often live nonproductive lives.

10

PROFIT FROM FAILURE

Penny Tip:

*Most people know what a ditch looks like
only after they fall into one.*

Most of us would look upon a gentleman driving a sanitation truck at 6:00am, and almost instinctively put him in a vacuum, capsulating his entire life to nothing more than failure. Given that sanitation or professions of custodial duties are the least regarded, our biggest fear is that one day our paths might lead us to such positions associated with, and socially deemed, "failure." We would most rather be unemployed than accept a position as a janitor or window-washer. Of course, the rationale is always, "There's nothing wrong with being a janitor; it's just not for me. I'm looking for 'something' in my field." Interestingly enough, that 'something' is usually no different than everybody else's 'something.' I've come to find out that 'something' is just a euphemism for 'a managerial position with a corner office.' Although you'd be pressed to find one who will verbalize it, most mull on one common thought, "An office job bespeaks my authority; my influence; my prestige; my power."

It's funny how societal perception has indoctrinated us to believe that positions and possessions define people. When we think of making ourselves valuable, we often reflect on positions and things. Some would argue that they consider intrinsic valuation, and not extrinsic motivations to determine their worth. Still, although some people are more substantive and less superficial than others are, no one is regarded as an exception to this notion. Subconsciously, we all seek for the material things to validate what we believe is our value. If we drive a very

85

nice new car, live in a beautiful condominium or house in the better part of town, and have lots of cash saved away, then we affirm our worth to others and ourselves. We carry ourselves as achievers.

Seldom, if ever, do we draw from our knowledge and abilities to substantiate our worth. If we live in a rat infested broom-closet with a negative cash flow driving our ends farther from meeting, and have to walk six miles every day to a minimum wage toilet-scrubbing position, we become very sheepish and subdued. The fact that we may be computer wizards and hidden physics geniuses, will not compel us to convince anyone of our worth. Although knowing how to do something with proficiency makes us feel good, it's simply not enough. We don't consider knowledge valuable, but that which is generated from having it. Why? Knowledge is just too abstract. You can't stick a price tag on the abstract. But you can certainly price a good suit.

It's very unlikely that a dishwasher will respond "I create mathematical formulas, solve statistical problems and write computer programs" when asked, "What do you do?" The likelihood that he will say, "I'm a dish-washer" is great. Naturally, we would not dream of mentioning to our "successful" friends how valuable we are. Instead, we would seize the opportunity to justify and explain how we landed such detested position, and rant on about how awful it is. We will even go as far as specifying the

86

particulars of our daily chores and responsibilities, as if anyone really wanted to know that liquid soap produces heavier suds than pulverized soap. Albeit our mathematical and computer wizardry is far more priceless and significant than our positions, most of us would feel rather foolish attempting to assert any personal worth at all. Certainly, a dish-scrubber can not have much valuation worth noting; otherwise he would not be scrubbing dishes. Right? Wrong.

I have come to find out that often times society attributes worth to the inutile and undeserving at the expense of the proficient and hard worker, the person in a "failure" position who has nothing with which to substantiate his worth. Based on his duties, society carelessly dismisses him as a loser, further promulgating "failure" upon anyone who performs those duties. Therefore, in subliminal ways we send the same message when we don't perform these duties for our own personal advantage. We would rather pay and often times 'overpay' for services we could perform ourselves.

If I told you that I steam clean my carpets, and wax my own hardwood floors very well, you'd probably say, "So what!" Most people don't find that newsworthy, let alone an activity worth mentioning. But considering that most people pay to have their carpets steam cleaned or hardwood floors waxed, these seemingly petty activities have business worth. That means I save the $300.00 that ordinarily would be allotted to pay for these services. Therefore, this "petty" chore saves me money. Do you tune-up your own car? Do you change the oil filter yourself? Do you change the bushings when the faucet drips, or do you call the plumber? Consider all the services for which we pay. Most of them we can perform ourselves, and save a lot of money. "But I don't know how to change my oil filter," some might argue. When you buy that $4 oil filter, it comes with step-by-step instructions and illustrations that a fourth grader can follow. So why pay a mechanic $79 plus tax to change your oil filter when he is going to resort to those very same instructions?

I'm not suggesting that you install your next clutch and rebuild your engine. The point is you must determine what you can and cannot do. Don't pay for things that you can do. Let us readjust your way of thinking. Forget about set societal standards. You are going to set your own standards for self worth, and you are going to live by them. From this day on, your feat will be **extracting worth from every "failure"activity.**

Take an inventory of all the activities you perform in the course of a day, week, month, and/or year:

- List every activity that you perform at your job, if you have one.
- List every activity that you perform at home.
- List every activity that you perform outdoors.
- List every activity that you perform indoors, other than your home.

Do not spare any details. It is important that you identify every activity, however insignificant or petty it may seem. Keep in mind that people spend most of their money in the "failure" industries, paying for the petty and insignificant things. After you've listed all your activities, identify all your "failure" activities. Go through the yellow pages, call companies that provide such services and get quotes for such services. You will be quite amazed how much of your money the so-called "failure" industry is gouging.

List every thing that you know how to do. Now, list every thing you would like to know how to do:

- Mechanical
- Academic
- Technical
- Recreational
- Domestic

Although your lists should be more detail specific, let's suppose your lists consist of the following:

KNOW HOW TO	WOULD LIKE TO LEARN
TYPE	COMPUTER SOFTWARES
WRITE	PROGRAMMING
FILE	GRAPHIC ARTS
DRAW/PAINT	

You are going to use what you know how to do as tools to help you learn those things that you would like to know how to do. Here's how. For the next six months, you are going to go to a computer store, computer programming firm, a graphic designing company, or any company that provides those services, and volunteer your services a few hours a week. That's right, volunteer. Offer your typing, writing, filing and drawing services. Your "paycheck" will be a wealth of knowledge and hands-on experience in that industry.

Likening this experience to any profession, we must be schooled in an area of business before we can practice skillfully in that field. Thus, in such undertaking, you should always look to learn from the experts. There is no better way to learn a thing than from the professionals, those who do it for a living. Volunteer and ask questions. Use what you have as a tool to learn from the best. In most cases,we have to pay for proper schooling and training. Take advantage of the opportunity.

Now go back to your list, and do it for real. Not only will you learn, but you will find it to be a lot of fun. You will also find that this experience will enhance what you do at your job, if you have one. If you don't have a job, 9 times out of 10, companies hire their volunteers. It's a win-win situation.

After you've learned an activity of your interest, don't stop there. Explore; learn something else to further enhance your duties. For instance, after you've learned how to use software programs such as Excel spreadsheets, Peachtree Accounting, Word for Windows. Master them! Learn how to develop formulas and macros. Read the "Help" from the menu toolbar. Oftentimes, the software's "Help" feature has demonstrations and examples to help you understand the concepts and procedures. You would be surprised how much of your job you can enhance by just using softwares. You can become extremely fast and efficient. Tasks that would ordinarily take two hours to

91

accomplish, you can accomplish in a matter of minutes by implementing macros.

Increase your value by increasing your knowledge and abilities. Don't just go to work to draw a paycheck. Work to increase your worth. Even if it is not the job of your choice, and you are actually quite dissatisfied, learn how to do something else that will enhance your abilities and value on the job.

The more you know, the less dispensable you become!

11

SAVE, INSURE, AND INVEST

Penny Tip:

A rich man is not rich because he spends it all!

By now, you probably have a good idea of how your system is going to work for you. But there is more. Diversify. It's a fancy word for "Don't keep all your goodies in one place." Spread your savings around. You've learned how to properly budget, save, and methods to increase your personal worth. Now its's time to invest and shelter your savings.

Savings Accounts, IRA's, and 401K's

You have already opened your savings account, and activated the monthly automatic transfer feature. PPC, as discussed earlier, will transfer 10%+ of your net income to your savings monthly. As you pay off your debt, the money that you have freed up goes into the savings, thus increasing your monthly savings. Remember to arrange the amount increase transfer with your bank. They will only transfer the amount you tell them and no more. It would be great if you can reach a 30% of net income. Of course, this will take paying off existing debt, bills and not replacing them with other debt.

Participate in tax shelter programs such as the IRA's, 401K's, insurance, and annuities. These are great because they are vehicles that shelter your savings from current taxation. With the traditional IRA, you can shelter up to $2,000.00(for singles) and $2,500.00(for married) from current taxation. This arrangement both encourages you to save and reduce your taxes. What a program! Once you have committed your funds to the IRA you may not withdraw until time of distribution, which is 59-1/2 years of age. If you withdraw, you will be required to pay a 10% penalty in addition to taxes. Distribution becomes mandatory at 70-1/2 years of age.

Keep in mind that you are saving for the long term. Therefore, this feature in the IRA should not be a deterrent. In fact, you should view it as a protective measure that will prevent you from spending your savings. You don't have to deposit only $2,000.00. You may deposit less or more. However, only $2000 will be tax deductible ($2500.00 if you're married).

There are other types of IRA's that you may want to peruse before making a final decision. Such are the Roth IRA and Education IRA. With the Roth IRA you are depositing dollars that have already been taxed. The advantage with the Roth IRA is that all appreciation is completely tax free at distribution, 59-1/2 years of age. The Education IRA is just that. Tax deductible funds that are put into an IRA for education. You can get more details at banks, broker dealers, and life insurance companies that offer these vehicles of investment.

Like the IRA's, 401K's are Qualified Programs, which means that they are approved tax deferred programs. The 401K is offered at your place of employment, and you are allowed to save up to 15% percent of your income on a tax deferred basis. In some cases your employer is willing to match your savings. If a 401K is offered at your job, find out the details of your employer's fund match. If I told you that I would give you $.50 for every dollar you save, how many dollars would you save? Or would you turn down the additional savings offered? I didn't think you would.

Annuities

An annuity is another tax-deferred program. However, there is a minimum savings requirement with an annuity, generally $1000.00. Also, unlike the IRA and 401K, there is no maximum savings limit. You may save beyond 15% of your income and/or $2000 tax deferred. There are several types of annuities. You can request literature on all types from most insurance companies. They will be more than happy to give you all the information and brochures you need.

Life Insurance

Life insurance is one of the financial vehicles least discussed, mainly because of what it represents: "In the event of my death...." Indeed it is a program designed in the event of death, but it carries more benefits than just a lump sum of money for beneficiaries. There are types of insurance that offer insurance coverage only, but life insurance has been enhanced to offer more than just coverage. Unfortunately, the thought of death keeps many from enjoying the benefits that come with having life insurance. Let us look at the various types of life insurance and their benefits.

- Term Life Insurance

Term insurance provides the insured with the peace of mind that his survivors will receive a lump sum of money at the point of his death. Term insurance is the least expensive initially when compared to other types of life insurance. The younger the insured, the lower the premium and the higher the coverage. The greatest advantage is the coverage. All premium payments are for insurance coverage only. Term does not appreciate in value nor does it accumulate any dividend and/or interest. This particular type of policy is excellent for young families, who are only looking for insurance coverage and have very limited funds. However, every renewal term, the premium will increase. As you get older, the more expensive the coverage becomes per unit of insurance. It is recommended that the term policy be upgraded to a cash value insurance at some point. Young families who need large coverage for the least amount of money should consider term insurance with a conversion provision.

This will allow them to convert to another type of insurance without having to re-qualify medically.

- Whole Life Insurance

Whole Life insurance appreciates in value over time. The policy builds what is called "cash value." Eventually, the policy builds enough cash value to continue making the premium payments for the life of the policy. Approximately by the fifteenth year, the average whole life typically appreciates enough cash value to continue the premium payment for the life of the policy. Some appreciate much sooner. It may take more or less years depending on the annual dividends. This is an excellent feature of the whole life insurance because it remains in effect without your having to continue to make payments out of pocket. And unlike the term insurance, the premium payments never increase. The dividends that accrue in the policy not only continue to make the premium payments, but continue building cash value in the policy.

The cash value is real money, which makes the policy an asset. Banks usually accept cash values in life insurance as collateral for loans. Which brings me to my next point. You can always borrow against your cash value if you need funds. And in the event that you want to surrender your policy, you may cash in your policy for its cash value. Depending on the length of time the policy has been in effect, surrendering a whole life can give you a cash return that exceeds the sum of all the payments you have made. Surely, you can see that this policy is ideal and excellent for everyone.

One of the biggest advantages of whole life insurance is the built in cash accumulation feature; and the IRS can't touch it if it bumped in to it. Should you decide to surrender the policy, only the appreciation is taxable at the point of surrender. Keep in mind that during the time the policy is in effect, it is appreciating much like the other tax shelter vehicles. It is accumulating compound interest on a tax-deferred basis. However, in the event of the death of the insured, all monies paid to the beneficiaries are non-taxable.

- Whole Life/Term Mix

There are some companies that offer a mixture of both term insurance and whole life, thereby allowing policy owners the advantages of both larger coverage amounts and cash value appreciation with a steady premium price. Of course this policy will not appreciate as much cash value as a pure whole life, but until you are able to get a pure whole life, this is an excellent alternative.

100

- Variable Insurance

Variable insurance is another type of whole life, which allows you to invest in equities such as stocks and bonds. Thus, this feature will appreciate or depreciate the cash value according to the performance of the equities.

Mutual Funds

Mutual funds are excellent investments for individuals who are interested in the stock market, but do not necessarily know how to go about investing in it, or are not aggressive investors. In a nutshell, investors send their money to an Investment Company, and the Investment Company turns around and invests in a mixture of securities such as stocks, bonds, and money markets. In essence, you are buying a unit of the Investment Company, which is invested in various vehicles. This takes the pressure of having to research and select the right stocks, bonds, etc...off of you. The Investment Company categorizes its various funds based on investment goals such as (growth, balanced, income, etc....), and invests in securities according to the goals set for each fund. As an investor, all you have to do is select from their menu of mutual funds based on your personal financial goals.

For example, Mr. Young, a 24-year-old single investor is interested in growth. He wants accelerated appreciation

101

in his portfolio. Given this fact, he will most likely select the growth funds, which are mostly invested in growth stocks (i.e. technology companies). Growth companies have the greatest likelihood for accelerated appreciation. However, Mr. Young should know that attached to the possibility of great gain is the possibility of great loss. The higher the gain possibility, the greater the risk for loss. After he is made aware of this information, he is still willing to invest in growth because he figures that he is young and can afford the risk.

Naturally, an older investor with a family may not be as interested in taking such risk. He may select a balanced fund, which targets both growth and income in which the risk is moderate.

Although there are never any guarantees in investments, mutual funds allow you to participate in the stock market with a degree of safeguard against capital loss. Since the funds invest in a variety of equities, a strong blow from an individual stock plummeting is absorbed by the diversification of the fund, thereby reducing your potential loss.

The investment industry has certain guidelines by which brokers can determine their customers' objectives. Based on these objectives, brokers suggest certain vehicles of investment that are designed to satisfy those objectives. A customer's objectives help the broker determine whether or not a particular investment is suitable for the customer. This is called **suitability analysis**. However, more often than brokerage firms will admit, suitability guidelines are not followed, and investors end up losing their hard-earned savings. Learn how to do your own suitability test. This way, when you make your investments, you know that the investment is indeed suitable for your needs. After all, you know your personal finances better than any broker, who is basically looking for the next big commission, does.

The following are definite investment objectives that you should know. After you become familiar with the objective categories, you can tailor your own plan based on personal goals.

- Capital Growth

Growth funds generally seek to invest in growth companies, which are typically expected to appreciate in value at a greater rate than the market in general. Because the main goal of growth companies is accelerated capital appreciation, they normally re-invest any profits back into the company. Thus, they seldom pay out dividends to shareholders.

103

- Income

Income funds concentrate on investments that yield income. The investment companies, typically referred to as funds, seek quality investments, companies that normally pay dividends to its shareholders. These companies are referred to as the 'blue chip' stocks. Income funds also look to invest in quality bonds and preferred stocks because of the potential for current income.

- Balanced

This fund is a combination of growth and income. While its goal is to achieve an income, it also looks to a value appreciation of capital. This mixture is appealing to investors who are interested in some capital appreciation, but would also like a consistent income from their investments.

- Tax Free

This fund's main objective is tax exemption. Some of its main investment vehicles are municipal securities and/or U.S. Government/Agency Securities (i.e. bills, bonds, and notes). This particular fund is most attractive to older investors.

- Money Market

The Money Market fund's main objective is current income with a high degree of liquidity. It is often used as an emergency savings account, and some even have a check writing feature. Money Market is one of the most widely invested funds because it functions much like a regular savings account. To meet its objectives, the fund may invest in short term vehicles such as U.S. Treasury bills, commercial paper, and certificates of deposits (CD).

While the aforementioned are some of the most common fund objectives, investment companies have gotten very creative. Some funds have mix-matched objectives to create very unique funds that appeal to the market. As stated earlier, your needs may vary slightly or widely from that of the rest of the population. It is to your advantage to understand the various goals and objectives of the funds offered.

There is practically a fund for every investment goal intended. You just have to pin point what your objectives are so that you can appropriately identify the right fund for you. Unless someone knows all the intricate details about your finances, which is as rare as hitting the lottery, no one can accurately assess what is best for you.

The following are some possible investment-objectives according to age groups.

Age range   **Objective**

20's   Aggressive Growth
                                 Some Income

30's   Capital Growth
                                 Income

Capital Growth
40's   Income

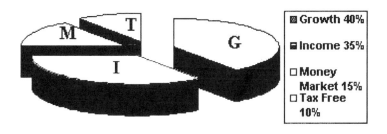

Tax Free
50's +   Income
Tax Free
Some Growth

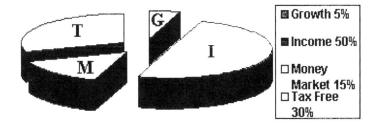

Stocks

Stocks do not have the same 'cushion' for loss as do mutual funds. Investing in stocks directly, puts you face to face with your gains and losses. So if you own 1000 shares of XYZ and it jumps three points in one day, you have made $3000. On the other hand, if it sinks three points, you have lost $3000. When you are investing in stocks, I highly recommend that you only do so after thorough research in that particular stock or investment.

Always be careful. It is easier to lose than it is to win. Your chances to lose by mistake are greater than your chances to win on purpose. This means you cannot afford to make any mistakes.

WARNING! Some of the biggest common mistakes are...

- **Investing based on Rumors**

Have you ever heard the old saying "bad news spreads like wild fire?" Well, this is true, particularly in the stock market. If the news is spreading, beware. Even if the rumor is positive information, it is most likely bad news, at least for you. Why? By the time this great tip hits your ears, the likelihood that the stock is on its way down, in many cases way way down, is more than great. The reality

108

is that in this industry, bad news is often dressed to look good. And the uninformed unassuming investor comes along and loses his pants and shirt.

Given that all news is "good," you have to decipher the 'real good news' from the 'bad good news.' It's sad to say, but nobody ever shares wealth with anyone. Think about it. If you knew the six winning numbers to the $150 million dollar lottery jackpot before the drawing, would you share those numbers with all your friends? I didn't think so, and most people would rather not share the jackpot either. In like manner, you will not be made privy to the 'real good news' in time to benefit from it. So what's the point of rumored "good news"? To influence the investor's behavior one way or another, always to the tipster's advantage.

For example, if a trader shorts 10,000 shares of XYZ at $60, do you think he will encourage you to buy more XYZ and drive the price above his mark of $60? No he won't. Even though you bought your 'smeasly' 200 shares at $65 two days ago, he will more readily talk you and others into selling your positions in XYZ at a loss. You sell. The price drops to $52. He and his other trader buddies buy in to cover their short positions. The price shoots up to $68. He makes an $8,000 profit, and you were left holding the bag with a loss of $1,000. Everything happened so fast, you can't even remember why you sold your 200 shares in the first place. Sounds familiar? This leaves us with a very logical inference. The "good" news that spreads is usually the bad one, at least for you.

Where were the rumors when the last merger was going to take place, before the stock shot up 9 points? Why were you not made privy to such great tip? You found out after it shot up 9 points, just in time to buy your few hundred shares only to see it plummet 10 points. And of course, it is not until after the stock opens way down, the next morning, that you find out that the companies have decided to end all negotiations. Where did that leave you?

- **Investing based on a 'recommended list'**

"Consider the source." Have you heard that before? A recommendation list is as good as the person or company who puts it together. Everyone has an opinion about a certain stock, and that opinion may or may not benefit you. Remember that nobody wants to share his wealth; and they definitely do not want to lose any. Perhaps the recommender has a large inventory on these stocks, and he knows that they are about to decline in value.

Given this fact, he is going to protect his investment at all cost. His opportunity to lock in a profit would be to pitch a 'recommended list' to the next unsuspecting foolish investor. He sells his "dead wood" stock to the ordinary Joe, and the next event is a cascade of falling prices. He makes all the money everyone else loses. Yes, such practices violate industry rules and regulations. But many traders and market makers, certainly not all, would rather take their chances with NASD and SEC sanctions than 'leave money on the table.'

The questions that you need to ask yourself are:

a) What is the recommender's interest in the stocks?
b) Does he have a substantial inventory that he's looking to get rid of?
c) Is he in some way associated with the issuer of the stock?
d) Does he have a track record for stock recommendation?
e) What is the technical or fundamental basis for recommendation?

While you may not get an answer to these questions, they are definitely worthy of consideration. Just as it is companies' responsibility to protect their interest, it is your responsibility to protect yours. It is a conflict of interest for a company to protect your interest at the expense of their bottom line.

Granted, there are some newsletters and research reports that offer sound advise and recommendation based on reliable fundamental information and technical analysis.

111

However, those sources are far, few, and in between. So remember, the only person on your team at all times is you. Ask questions. Research! If you do not get an answer to your satisfaction, do not invest.

- **investing because my broker advised**

You've probably heard the two-cent broker's stale line, "I bought some for myself, and I got my mom in it." Well, I suppose if his house cat had a tax ID number, he'd throw in a few dollars for him too. If he and all his constituents are so well invested in this such 'great' stock, what's going to happen when it's no longer an attractive stock, and it's time to sell? I guess he'll be pulling your hair to sell his first.

Clearly, you can see the conflict of interest? Also, we must consider what the broker's real interest is at all times. Commissions! Chances are that he doesn't own the stock after all, and he's just creating a ploy to get you to buy. He could care less whether you have a great investment or not. He doesn't get paid on the quality of the stock he sells, nor on the rate of return on your account, but on the total dollar amount invested, which leads me to another important fact you should know.

A broker's commission is typically anywhere from 2 to 5 percent of total amount invested, with a minimum of approximately $25.00. If you had to make a choice between two excellent stocks, ABC @ $5 a share and DEF @ $31 a share, which are both projected to double in value within six months, what do you suppose your broker would recommend?

1000 ABC @ $5.00=	$ 5,000.00
Commission ($5000 x 5%)	**$ 250.00**
	$ 5,250.00

-or-

1000 DEF @ $31.00=	$31,000.00
Commission ($31,000 x 5%)	**$ 1,550.00**
	$32,550.00

Your broker would most likely recommend DEF @ $31 for a commission of $1550.00.

Be mindful that brokers are just brokers and nothing more. Their licenses afford them the right and responsibility to charge a fee for executing a customer's buy or sell order. They are not licensed investment advisors. And making an investment advisor out of your broker is an injustice to both you and your broker. He is there to provide you with public information in hopes that you make an educated decision as it pertains to your investment. Once you have made a decision, he will execute your orders, and on to the next customer.

There are some brokers who are licensed as investment advisors, but most are not. In fact, you'll be hard pressed to find a broker who can read a graph or a balance sheet. Indeed, many times brokers introduce certain investment vehicles to customers as buy opportunities, but it is based on research and/or information disseminated by the investment advisor at their firm, not their own personal analysis. In most cases, brokers push certain stocks because the traders or market makers at their firm urge them to. When a trader yells across the floor, "I'm heavy in XYZ, I need some tickets in that stock," the flurry that brokers create, pitching the stock, is deafening.

Should you want advice, make sure that your representative has the Series 65 license, the Investment Advisor license, otherwise 'puppetry' advice is the best you're going to get. Know that there are excellent brokers who truly want to give their clients the best kind of service there is to offer. Unfortunately, most often they are not knowledgeable and/or experienced enough to assume that role of an advisor.

- **investing because of very low prices**

Never buy a stock only because it has a low price. A high percentage of very low priced stocks go lower. Some even go right off the charts. That is not to say that all low priced stocks are bound to fail. There are many excellent low priced securities worth your investment, but you must be informed about the history of the stock's growth rate. You can always get copies of company earnings and news releases from the actual companies. Hopefully, a seed of caution has been planted in your investment approach.

12

TRADE FOR PROFIT

Penny Tip:

Money works for nobody.
You have to do the work yourself!

With most households getting actively involved in the stock market as a means of increasing personal income, trading, although still a cloistered profession, must be included as an intricate part of the average household's financial activities. More people are putting on the hat of "the trader" in order to advance their economic position. And given this fact, let us explore strategies of trading for profit.

This will require additional work on your part. That's right, you're going to do a little work. Whoever said "let your money go to work for you!" must have been in a deep dream. Certainly this concept has been around for a while. Why hasn't it worked for you? After all, you have wanted financial success for a long time. Fortunately, in the process of building your empire you have come to the realization that any and every inch of progress is a direct result of your decisions and actions. Nothing is going to happen to your advantage without your putting forth effort.

Thinking that your money is going to work for you is as idealistic as suddenly waking up in a pool of cash. You are the only one who is going to have to make the money, do all the research regarding the investment vehicle, make all the decisions regarding where your money will go, and for how long. After that, you are the one who is going to have to execute every decision. Money works for nobody, and it certainly isn't loyal to anyone. Money doesn't care in whose pocketbook, tabletop, or account it sits.

Have you ever put a rake on the front lawn, and come to it the next morning to find all the leaves raked? I didn't think so. If you put your money in a stock that is heading up, it is not going to get out on its own when the stock reaches its peak to allow you the advantage of a profit. Likewise, if you put the same money in a stock that is about to dive to the lowest lows, it is not going to jump out on its own to keep you from losing your life's savings.

This is the problem that has plagued many investors, and kept them from financial gain. They have substituted fine-tuning their analytical skills for the ideology that someone or something else is going to do the work for them. In this case, that something is money. In subscribing to this concept, they not only rid themselves of responsibility, but they relinquish all control over their personal finances. And when there is no control, there is no discipline, and the outcome is always uncertain.

In a nutshell, trading is buying low and selling higher to capture a profit. When you trade, you must be in control at all times. You determine how much money to put in a particular stock, and for what period of time. Your timing decisions will determine how much gain you will have. Money is definitely your vehicle, but your abilities to read and analyze graphs and charts, identify market trends, and determine execution times are the key elements in making a substantial profit in the stock market. Some other key factors to watch include, but are not limited to:

- Price Range: High/Lows
- Trend: Up & Down pattern
- Relative Strength: Overbought/Oversold
- MACD   Buy/Sell Signals
- FS/SS Stochastics   Buy/Sell Signals
- Shares Traded: Heavy/Thin
- Volume: Supply/Demand
- Company News: Financials/Developments

- **Price Range**
Figure 1

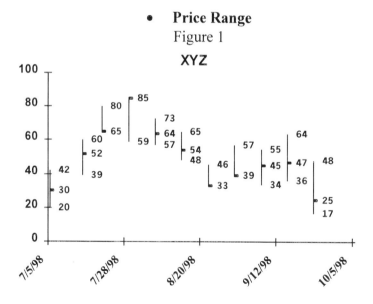

XYZ

During the course of a day, a stock trades within a price range. In the case of figure 1, on July 5, 1998, stock XYZ traded all day long between prices of 20 and 42. This means 20 was the lowest price and 42 the highest price. The goal is to buy as close to the lowest point and sell as close to the highest point. The difference between the buy and sell points is your profit. If you buy 500 shares of XYC at 35 ¼ and sell at 36 1/8 that same day, your profit is 7/8 of a point or $437.50.

Example:

Sell 500 x $36 1/8=	$18062.50
Buy 500 x $35 1/4=	$17625.00
Profit	**$ 473.50**

You are not limited to the number of times you may repeat this pattern. If you repeat this buy and sell pattern three times a day, your profit will be $1,312.50 for the day. Your profit taking depends greatly on your ability to capture profits quickly and repeat the process. Remember, when investing, "time" is everything; but when trading, "timing" is everything.

- **Trend**
Figure 2

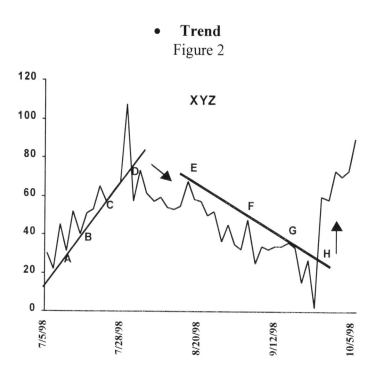

The **Trend** of a stock is basically the direction in which it is going. Three points that connect usually establish the trend in a straight line. The direction of this line will indicate whether the stock is heading up or down. Figure 2 illustrates a trend line established by points A, B, and C. This trend is upward, therefore it can be estimated that it's on its way up. Figure 2 also illustrates a downward trend established by points E, F, and G.

123

The upward trend is broken at point D. It is at this point that the stock reverses its direction. Whenever the stock goes below the upward trend line that has already been established, it is no longer on an upward trend. It is heading lower. Likewise, the downward trend is broken at point H. At this point, the stock has reversed the downward direction, and is heading upward above the downward trend line.

Clearly, the trend line is instrumental in allowing for a general view of where the stock is headed. Never ever ignore the trend line.

• **RELATIVE STRENGTH INDEX**

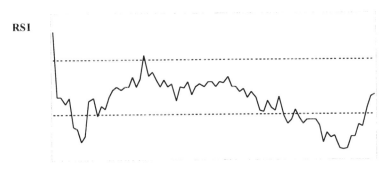

The **Relative Strength** is the performance of a stock in relation to the overall performance of the market. Since relative strength gauges both the market of the individual security compared to that of all other stocks in general,

124

it maintains a pulse for the activity of the stock at all times. Thus, the Relative Strength Index is able to indicate when a stock is reaching its point of saturation, overbought and oversold levels. Once the stock reaches either level, it usually makes a direction reversal. For instance, when a stock has an upward relative strength, this means that the stock has a capacity for accumulation or buying. When it reaches the overbought point on the index (the top dotted line), it is an indication that buying will slow down, and selling is imminent.

- **MACD**

Moving Average Convergence/Divergence

MACD
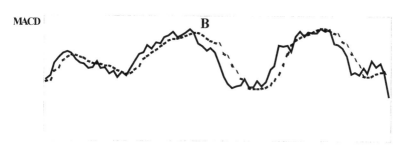

MACD is another excellent indicator for identifying trends, buy, and sell signals. A **Moving Average** keeps track of all the closing prices over a period of time. The Moving Average Convergence Divergence (MACD) basically takes two separate moving averages and keeps

125

track of the market fluctuations. At whatever points both moving averages meet, a 'buy' or 'sell' signal is established. Notice in the graph above, at the point when the dotted moving average goes below the solid moving average, the stock is in a 'buy' mode. Therefore, the 'buy' signal is established at the point when both averages meet (point A). Whenever, the dotted moving average goes above the solid moving average, the stock is in a 'sell' mode. The 'sell' signal is established when both averages meet (point B).

- **10 week Moving Average (MA)**

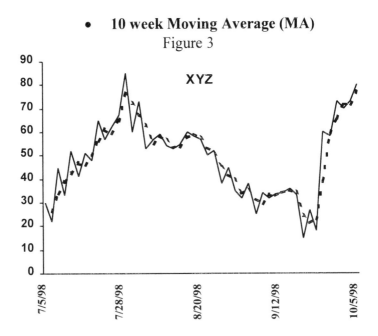

Figure 3

10 Week MA is another moving average that averages the closing price of a stock over a period of 10 weeks. This moving average is for short-term traders, because it evaluates a shorter period of time than does the 30 Week MA.

- **Stochastics**

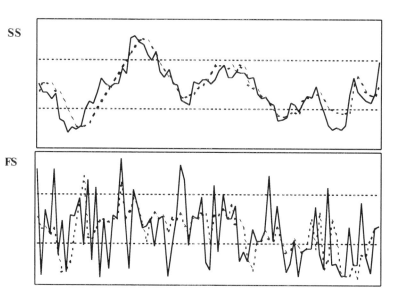

Stochastic is like the MACD, in that it serves as a buy and sell indicator. The stochastic is an overbought and oversold oscillator, and a short-term trend indicator. There are two types of Stochastic, the Fast Stochastic (FS) and the Slow Stochastic (SS). Without getting too technical, when the dotted line goes below the solid line, it is a buy

127

signal. On the converse, when the dotted line goes above the solid line it is a sell signal. The FS has faster buy and sell fluctuations, more commonly used for day trading. The SS usually follows the FS.

- **VOLUME**

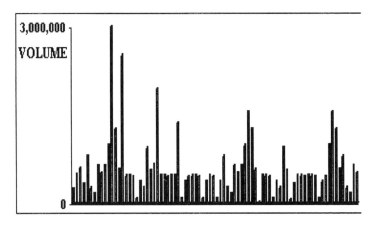

While **Volume** doesn't establish up/down trends or buy/ sell signals, it indicates accumulation. Usually, if there is great volume in a stock, it points to a great probability that there are many people buying the stock. When there are lots of buyers, it is safe to assume that there is great demand, and the price of the stock may be going up.

However, there are times when volume increases do not foretell a price increase. Sometimes a great price drop in the stock can cause a volume increase. When investors are looking to sell their stock at once, it causes the price to fall. Even in the case of a great sell-off, there are always buyers who will buy the massive inventory being sold. This being the case, volume is not an indication of price increase, but stock activity.

Volume is a great tool for studying the potential of a security, but it doesn't stand alone. It has to be studied in direct correlation with other indicators for it to be most effective.

- **Shares Traded**

Shares Traded is the amount of shares bought and sold in the course of a trade day. There is no set amount of shares that deems a stock thinly or heavily traded. The stocks that trade a small number of shares compared to the market are considered thinly traded securities, and do not have a lot of activity in the course of a day. On the converse, the ones that trade a large number of shares are considered heavily traded, and the activity is great. Since thinly traded stocks do not have a lot of activity, and usually few market makers, it is likely that there will be no great price movement in the stock. The stocks with great activity can be expected to have price movements in the course of a day.

As a trader looking to capture a profit, it is best to stay away from the thin securities. The heavy ones offer a better opportunity for price movement in which one can grab a gain. It is possible to buy at 18 and sell at 18 3/4 in a stock that has great activity. This possibility not only evaporates but is almost an impossibility when dealing with thinly traded stocks.

- **Company News**

Company News keeps the public informed. Issues such as company financial standing, service and product developments, affect stock prices. It is common knowledge that good news will cause a stock price to go up, while bad news will cause it to go down. It is important that the investor always analyze the information and/or news on which he is relying to trade a stock in relation to the stock performance.

Let's look at a case. If a company releases news that its stock's earnings growth rate tripled, this is certainly excellent information that would cause any good stock to go up. If in spite of such great news the stock price doesn't move and the volume decreases, this may serve as a red flag that something is seriously wrong. It is probably a good idea to sell that stock. Surely, you understand why.

If you push a cart with all your might and it doesn't move, it is safe to assume that there is an opposing force of equal magnitude that is keeping it from going forward. What do you think will happen to your cart if you stop pushing and instead another force joins with the already existing opposing force? You can rest assured that the cart will not be going forward, but backward.

Make sure that you capture the benefits of good news. The best time to sell is when all is well. Don't be greedy. As long as you are ahead, you win. Sell when the news is good. Don't sit around waiting for more good news in hopes for a greater price increase. The next company news release may be the news that swallows up all your capital.

Let's put it all together in analyzing the following graphs. Which one would you trade?

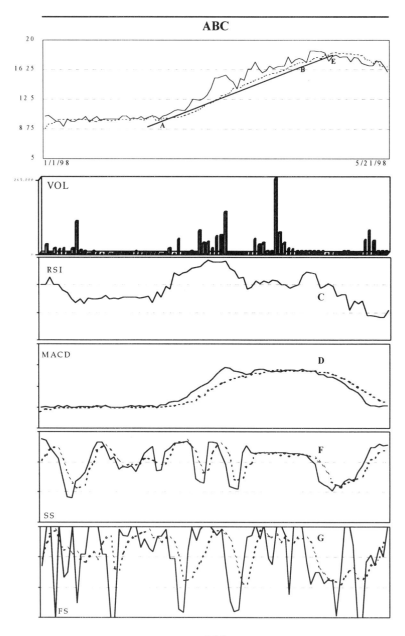

132

Line AB

This trend line has been upward, and was established on the third point. The overall price direction was up, and should have been considered for purchase until the price broke below trend line.

Point C

Although the relative strength trend is upward, it has been at the overbought level (the top of the scale) for a while. This usually warns that there may be a sell-off in the stock, which may cause the price to drop. The stock may not have more strength to go too much higher, and may lose steam instead. At this point, it's the third time the relative strength goes below the overbought level. This usually indicates a downward trend. So watch for a turn around in the stock price.

Point D

The dotted moving average has clearly gone over the solid moving average on the MACD scale. At this point, a "sell" signal is established. The stock price is headed lower.

133

Point E

The 10 Week MA has gone over the actual price. This indicates that the price has lost upward strength to stay above the moving average. Again, the price is headed lower.

Points F

The dotted line has crossed above the solid line, and a sell signal has been established.

Points G

The dotted line has crossed above the solid line, and a sell signal has been established.

Moreover, the volume is minimal. There are not too many buyers accumulating shares of this particular stock. Proceed with caution, and be careful. This usually means that there is very little demand.

Note: There is great possibility that the company has news that will cause the stock to drop.

Tip: Given that the position of the indicators point to a 'sell', the price range during the day becomes essential. You have already determined that the stock is a 'sell'. Therefore selling closest to the day's highest price is your goal. However, don't spend too much time trying to sell at the highest price when it is clear that the stock is going lower. You may lose all your profit.

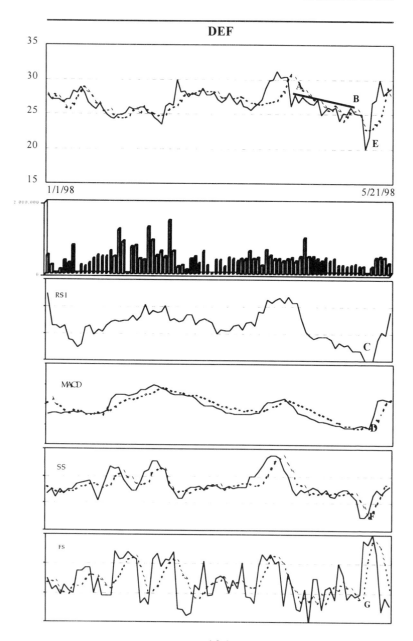

Line AB

This trend line is downward, and was established on the third point. The overall price direction is downward, and all indicators point to a "sell." Therefore, it should not be bought until indicators turn around.

Point C

The relative strength is upward, and it has not reached the overbought level. In fact, it is closer to the oversold level. This is good because it means it has quite a ways to go up before it reaches the overbought point. The stock has more strength to go higher, and the likelihood is that it will.

Point D

The dotted moving average has gone under the solid moving average on the MACD scale. At this point, a "buy" signal is established. The stock price is headed higher.

Point E

The 10 Week MA has gone under the price. This indicates

that the price has gained upward strength to stay above the moving average. The price is headed higher, and it's the best time to buy it.

Point F

The dotted line has crossed below the solid line, and a buy signal has been established.

Point G

The dotted line has crossed below the solid line, and a buy signal has been established.

At Point E, the Volume is not excessive; but the next three days indicates accumulation, especially at the point when the price has clearly broken above the 10 week MA. This means that although the stock is a good buy at Point E, it's a better and safer buy three days later because all indicators are consistent with a buy. Three days after Point E, there are buyers accumulating shares of this stock. This is good because there is demand. The greater the demand for the stock, the greater the likelihood that the price will go higher.

Note: Chances are the company has good news.

Tip: Again, the price range for the stock during the day is very important. Once the indicators point to a 'buy', try to buy as close to the lowest price to maximize your profit. Don't wait too long because a stock that is positioned to go higher usually does, and will leave you in the dust.

As you have analyzed for yourself, At Point E, DEF is better poised for purchase than is ABC. All the indicators suggest that the stock price will progress to higher levels. Know that there are exceptions to the rules. At times, stocks that have downward trend-lines, moving averages that signal "sells," and relative strengths that scream "way overbought," go way up. This obviously defies all the indicators, but you have no way of projecting an upward movement other than a very 'wild guess'. However, a 'wild guess' is not your purpose in the pursuit of financial betterment. Leave that to lottery. Your purpose is to reach a high degree of certainty that a profit will be the outcome based on the indicators.

Plummeting Stocks

A red flag to look for is the plummeting stock. Oftentimes, stocks that drop in price are seen as good buys because they are cheaper. BEWARE! When a stock plummets abruptly, it is almost a sure bet that it will go down further. Let's look at the following example.

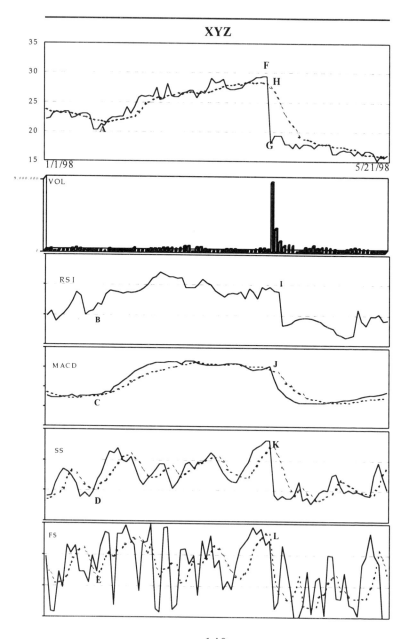

XYZ

Be extremely careful, if not skeptical, when buying stocks that have plummeted abruptly. Most traders/investors may consider a stock that has taken a 'nose-dive' very appealing. Don't be fooled. There are many stocks that drop in price drastically and immediately become a 'hot pick' because of their cheaper prices, but even cheap stocks deserve to be analyzed. A stock that was a good buy at $30 isn't necessarily a good buy at $10.

Let us look closely at the graph above. XYZ was a good buy in January when the stock was trading around $21 7/8 (Point A). The stock was on an upward trend, the relative strength (Point B) was heading higher, and the dotted lines went under the solid lines on the MACD Index (Point C), 10Wk MA (Point A), and Stochastics (Points D and E). For the next four months the stock continued to increase until April. On April 1, XYZ had a closing price of 29 1/6 (Point F). That day, the stock traded between 28 7/8 (low) and 29 1/8 (high). The following day, the stock dropped 10 11/16 points, 36% of its value, to close at 18 3/8 (Point G). All day, it traded between 17 (low) and 19 ½ (high). After reaching a low of 17, it finally closed at 18 3/8. At this point, the stock was no longer a good buy even though the price was 36% cheaper. All the indicators at that point were suggesting that the price was going lower: the relative strength (Point I) was heading downward; the dotted lines had crossed over the solid lines on the MACD (Point J), 10 Wk MA (Point H), and Stochastics (Points K and L). Clearly not a time to buy.

The most important thing to keep in mind about a plummeting stock is the 'false bottom'. Days following the drastic drop, the stock tends to suggest that it has reached its bottom and it is back on its way up. BEWARE! Notice how the stock starts to go up for the next few days; it climbs from 18 3/8 to 19 1/16. Most do this, thus leading the trader/investor to believe that the worst is over. However, after the slight gain, the stock continues to fall even lower. By May, the stock has reached a low $15. And quite frankly, the indicators tell me that the price will either continue to go lower or stay in that pit for a very long time. Therefore, unless all the indicators say "buy," stay away from plummeting stocks.

While it used to be the case that you needed a broker to transact a trade in your investment portfolio, that is not is not so anymore. Technology has made it so that investors can execute their own transactions without the use of a broker. The mechanics of trading is as simple as using the ATM's. Most brokerage houses use some sort of automated system that allows you to trade the stock that you want to buy or sell. You may specify the number of shares, and at what price you are willing to transact. For this commodity, the investor pays a very low flat fee of anywhere between $8-$25 a trade. The $300 and upward commission per trade is a thing of the past. Thank God for the added savings.

If your initial investment in your trading account is **$10,000**, you can...

B/S	STOCK	SHARES	PRICE	FLAT FEE	CASH BALANCE
Buy	XYZ	300	26 1/4	$12.00	$2,113.00
Sell	XYZ	300	27 1/2	$12.00	$10,351.00
Profit:		**$351.00**			
Buy	ABC	500	16 1/2	$12.00	$1,738.00
Sell	ABC	500	17 1/8	$12.00	$10,288.50
Profit:		**$288.50**			
Buy	DEF	325	28 3/4	$12.00	$644.25
Sell	DEF	325	30	$12.00	$10,382.25
Profit:		**$382.25**			
Your Gross Profit for the day is :					**$1,021.75**

Consider the kind of profit you will have if you repeat this pattern 10 times a day or even every other day. You determine how many times you are going to buy and sell during the course of the day. Also, you may want to increase the number of shares you trade once your portfolio starts to appreciate in value. If your trades were in denominations of a 1,000, your profit would be $3053.00 for the day; not bad for additional income.

Dabbling in the stock market is no longer an avenue traveled only by sophisticated investors and industry professionals. Wall Street has become a familiar street to the common household, and rightfully so. Investing has proven to be a lucrative tool with which many have been able to supplement income.

13

ASSURED RICHES

Penny Tip:

Save your pennies and bank your millions!

1 PENNY TIP:

Always honor your word.
If you breach your own word,
who won't you breach?

In the financial industry "your word is your bond." If you breach your own word, you will breach a contract and infringe upon others' rights. Thus, more valuable than money is "your word." Keep it.

2 PENNY TIP:

Don't run away from creditors;
pay your debts off.

Debt does not "go away"; it's paid off. Remember that a delinquent account decreases your credit, and increases your debt in arrears. So don't be derelict in duty; pay up.

3 PENNY TIP:

Responsible behavior
will afford you great
rewards.

Honored commitments are rewarded. When you fulfill your duties and responsibilities, creditors extend preferential courtesies, favors, discounts, and sometimes gifts.

4 PENNY TIP:

Take from Peter to pay Paul,
only if it's going to advance
your financial position!

Don't finagle and maneuver just to avoid payments or beat deadlines. Use the financial strategies availed to you to consolidate your debts and lower your interest charges. These financial arrangements are offered to facilitate your payments, not to avoid them.

5 PENNY TIP:

*If you won't pay
yourself for what you do,
why should anyone else?*

Whenever we contract the services of a plumber or an electrician, we never object to his quotation of $30 an hour. In fact, we accept it as a bargain. Yet when we have to give a quote for our services or time, that figure always falls somewhere between a "shoulder shrug" of uncertainty and "free." Determine what your services are worth and don't be afraid to state it.

6 PENNY TIP:

*Buy the shrimp dinner,
only if it costs less
than your income
minus expenses.*

Remember that if your purchases for personal enjoyment exceed the amount of your available funds you are living beyond your means. Cut down!

7 PENNY TIP:

Save NOW!

If you're still living at home, have a job, and don't have any financial responsibilities, save your money. Take advantage of your immediate circumstances while you can. It's not always going to be that easy.

8 PENNY TIP:

Sort and process twice a month, and keep a running balance.

Writing a check without ascertaining the actual balance in the account is asking for trouble. Keep in mind that it is illegal to write a check without having the money in the account. Determine your current account balance by subtracting all previously written checks, withdrawals, and bank charges from your beginning balance. Only after you have established that figure may you write additional checks and/or withdraw.

9 PENNY TIP:

Define the controls for
your financial landscape;
establish and practice them.

Financial success requires lifetime discipline, not a "get rich quick" trick. Comport yourself like a money manager, and you'll have plenty to manage. Don't deviate from your system. Establish it, and stick to it.

10 PENNY TIP:

Most people know what
a ditch looks like only
after they fall into one.

Only your personal experiences can prompt you to make certain changes in your financial practices, not anyone else's anecdotes. I can share with you countless stories with dreadful consequences, but that's not going to make a difference in your life. One thousand stories won't motivate you to change your practices, but one experience can. Stories don't prompt people to change, experiences do. Learn from your experiences.

11 PENNY TIP:

*A rich man is not rich
because he spends it all!*

The difference between the rich and the poor is that the rich spend their money on some of what they want and invest the rest, while the poor spend their money on most of what they want and save nothing. If you want to have money, save money.

12 PENNY TIP:

*Money works for nobody.
You have to do the work yourself!*

If you let money work for you, you will relinquish control to it, and whatever you gain or lose will suit you just fine!

13 PENNY TIP:

*Save your pennies,
and bank your millions.*

A wise old woman once said, "The only people who start at the top are gravediggers." There is great honor in starting from the bottom and building to the top. An earned penny dignifies a man, while found millions often raises questions about his hand. Save your pennies, and bank your millions.

For upcoming publications and other merchandise, visit us at our website:

www.ariassfortune.com

where everybody visits for up-to-date information on financial markets and news. Come see what industry experts, market analysts, and information specialists have to offer you.

ARIASS FORTUNE, INC.

We Make It!

ABOUT THE AUTHORS

HELSA ARIASS

Helsa Ariass, born and raised in New York City, is a graduate of UCLA. During her graduate studies, she focused in the area of securities research analysis, financial markets, and regulations. As a Financial and Operations Principal (Series 27), General Securities Principal (Series 24), and Equities Trader (Series 55) registered with the National Association of Securities Dealers, Helsa served as Director of Compliance and Compliance Officer for several investment firms in California, New York, Utah, Colorado, and Arizona. Currently, she is President and CEO of Ariass Fortune, Inc., a professional equities trading firm. Helsa appears in listings such as Standard & Poor's, Dunn & Bradstreet, and Strathmore's Who's Who.

GLAURYS ARIASS

Glaurys Ariass, born and raised in New York City, received her degree from UCLA. During her graduate studies, she specialized in the area of securities finance, corporate and proprietary interests. As a Financial and Operations Principal (Series 27), General Securities Principal (Series 24), and Equities Trader (Series 55) registered with the National Association of Securities Dealers, Glaurys served as Director of Proprietary Finance and Financial Officer for several investment firms in California, New York, Utah, and Arizona. She is also a licensed Life, Health & Disability Insurance Agent/Broker with the states of California. With nine years of experience as a securities trader, she is currently Vice President and CFO of Ariass Fortune, Inc., a professional equities trading firm. Glaurys appears in listings such as Standard & Poor's and Dunn & Bradstreet.